Sally Morgan was born in Perth, Western Australia, in 1951. She completed a Bachelor of Arts degree at The University of Western Australia in 1974. She also has post-graduate diplomas from The Western Australian Institute of Technology (now Curtin University of Technology) in Counselling Psychology and Computing and Library Studies. She is married with three children.

As well as writing, Sally Morgan has also established a national reputation as an artist. She has works in numerous private and public collections both in Australia and North America. Her first book, *My Place,* became and instant national best-seller, and has been published to considerable acclaim in Britain and North America. *Wanamurraganya: The Story of Jack McPhee* is her second book.

Arthur Corunna's Story

Arthur Corunna's Story

SALLY MORGAN

edited by Barbara Ker Wilson

FREMANTLE ARTS CENTRE PRESS

First published 1990 by
FREMANTLE ARTS CENTRE PRESS
1 Finnerty Street (PO Box 891), Fremantle
Western Australia, 6160.

Original unabridged edition of *My Place* published 1987.

Editor Barbara Ker Wilson.
Designed by John Douglass.
Production Manager Helen Idle.

Typeset in 11/12pt Clearface by Typestyle, Perth, Western Australia and printed on 100gsm Woodfree by Tien Wah Press (Pte.) Ltd, Singapore.

National Library of Australia
Cataloguing-in-publication data

Morgan, Sally, 1951-
   Arthur Corunna's story.

   ISBN 0 949206 77 6.

   1. Morgan, Sally, 1951 -   - Family. [2]. Aborigines,
   Australian - Biography - Juvenile literature. [3].
   Aborigines, Australian - Women - Biography - Juvenile
   literature. [4]. Aborigines, Australian - Social life and
   customs - Juvenile literature. I. Wilson, Barbara Ker,
   1929-   . II. Morgan, Sally, 1951-   . My Place. III.
   Title. IV. Title: My Place.

994.0049915

To My Family

How deprived we would have been
if we had been willing
to let things stay as they were.
We would have survived,
but not as a whole people.
We would never have known
our place.

ACKNOWLEDGEMENTS

Fremantle Arts Centre Press receives financial assistance from the Western Australian Department for the Arts.

Some of the personal names included in this book have been changed, or only first names included, to protect the privacy of those concerned.

CONTENTS

1

I'M GOING TO WRITE A BOOK

'I'm going to write a book.' It was the beginning of 1979, a good time for resolutions.

'Another new scheme, eh?' my mother asked sarcastically. She was used to my wild ideas.

'Not just a scheme this time, Mum. This time I'm really going to do it.'

'A children's book?'

Mum had started collecting children's books for my daughter and son ever since they were born.

'Nope. A book about our family history.'

'You can't write about our family,' she spluttered. 'You don't know anything.'

'Aah, but I'm going to find out, aren't I?'

In fact, I had longed to find out the whole truth about our family ever since I first learned of our Aboriginal background. When we were children, my mother and Nan had always told my two brothers and two sisters and me that we were Indian. It wasn't until I was at high school that I discovered we were really Aboriginal.

We all used to live in a rented house in a working-class suburb of Perth. I still thought of it as our family home, and even though I was married, with a home of my own, I saw my family nearly every day. There were such strong bonds between us it was impossible for me not to want to see them. Just as well Paul, my husband, was the uncomplaining sort! Though in fact he fitted into our family very well.

My father, who never recovered from his wartime experiences — he was in the army and became a prisoner-of-war — died when I was nine. Mum was left with five kids to rear. I was the eldest. My grandmother lived with us. We had a warm, happy childhood with plenty of loving and plenty of laughter.

But I shall never forget the day I came home from school to find Nan sitting at the kitchen table, crying. I froze in the doorway. I'd never seen her cry before.

'Nan...what's wrong?' I asked.

She lifted up one arm and thumped her clenched fist hard on the table. 'You kids don't want me, you want a white grandmother. I'm black! Do you hear, black, black, black!' With that, she pushed back her chair and hurried to her room. I never did find out what had upset her so. I think it was all to do with us growing up and not being little kids any longer.

I remember how I continued to stand in the doorway. I could feel the strap of my heavy school-bag cutting into my shoulder, but I was too stunned to remove it.

For the first time in my fifteen years, I was conscious of Nan's colouring. She was right, she wasn't white. Well, I thought logically, if she wasn't white, then neither were we. What did that make us, what did that make me? I had never thought of myself as being black before.

I was very excited by my new heritage, and ever since that day I had been trying to find out more about our family. My mother wouldn't openly admit the fact that we were part-Aboriginal until I was at University — and then the truth slipped out by accident in the middle of a conversation one day. Since then, she'd become almost as eager as I was to find out about our people. She and I had many small conversations about the past, but we tended to cover the same ground.

Sometimes Mum would try to get Nan to talk. One day I heard Nan shout, 'You're always goin' on about the past these days, Gladys. I'm sick of it. It makes me sick in here' — she pointed to her chest. 'My brain's no good, Glad, I can't 'member!'

Mum gave up easily. 'She's been like that all her life,' she said. 'She'll never change. When I was little, I used to ask about my father, but she wouldn't tell me anything. In the end, I gave up.'

'Who was your father?' I asked her.

'I don't know,' she replied sadly. 'Nan just said he was a white man who died when I was very small.'

I felt sad then. I promised myself I would find out who her father was. She had a right to know.

As a matter of fact, Nan had let a few things drop recently, ever since her brother Arthur had started to make regular visits. He was keen to see more of Nan now they were both getting older. And he was very fond of Mum.

'Who is he?' I asked Mum when I found him parked in front of the TV one day with a huge meal on his lap.

'You remember. Arthur, Nan's brother. When you were little he visited us a couple of times.'

I cast my mind back and suddenly recalled how he'd visited us ages ago, when my father was still alive. Suddenly I saw him as he had been so many years before: very tall and dark, with the biggest smile I'd ever seen.

'Is he her only brother?' I asked.

Mum laughed. 'The only one I know of. He's a darling old bloke, a real character.'

'Mum,' I said slowly, 'you don't think he could tell us about the past? About Nan, I mean.'

'I think he could, if we can get him to talk. He tells some wonderful stories.'

It took a while for me to get close to Arthur. He loved Mum, but he was wary of the rest of us. He wasn't quite sure what to make of us, and he wasn't quite sure what we made of him. If he had known just how curious we were about him and his past, he would probably have been scared right off.

On one visit he did provide us with a vivid picture from the past: some old photographs of Nan, taken in the 1920s. Nan had always refused to allow any of us to take her photograph. It was exciting to see her as a young woman. She, however, was not impressed.

When Arthur was around, Nan was frightened of what he might tell us. 'Don't listen to him,' she told us one day when he was halfway through a story about the old times. 'He's only a stupid old man. What would he know? He'll tell you wrong!'

'Is she goin' on again?' Arthur asked Mum.

'You silly old man,' Nan grumbled. 'Who do you think you are? Nobody's interested in your stories. You're just a silly old blackfella.'

'Aah, you'll have to think of a better name than that to call me.' He smiled. 'I'm proud of bein' a blackfella. Anyway, you're a blackfella yourself.'

Nan was incensed. No one had called her a blackfella for years.

'I may be a blackfella,' she said, 'but I'm not like you. I dress decent and I know the right way to do things. Look at you, a grown man and you got your pants tied up with a bit of string!'

'Now, Nanna,' Mum said in her Let's Be Reasonable voice, 'Arthur is your only brother, yet whenever he comes here you pick a fight with him. You're both getting old, it's time you made up.'

'We don't want to hear his stories,' Nan said forcefully. 'He wasn't the only one hard done by.'

'No, he wasn't,' Mum replied, 'but at least he'll talk about it. You won't tell us anything. We're your family, we've a right to know.'

'Glad, you and Arthur are a good pair, you don't know what a secret is.'

'It's not a matter of secrets, Nan,' Mum reasoned. 'You seem to be ashamed of your past, I don't know why. You've never told me anything, never let me belong to anyone. All my life, I've wanted a family, but you won't even tell me about my own grandmother. At least Arthur tells me something.'

Nan opened her mouth to reply, but Arthur cut in. 'If you don't go, Daisy, I'll tell them your Aboriginal name.'

Nan was furious. 'You wouldn't!' she fumed.

'Too right I will,' said Arthur.

Nan knew when she was beaten, and stormed off.

'What is it?' both Mum and I asked excitedly after she'd gone.

'No, I can't tell you,' he said. 'I'd like to, but Daisy should tell you herself. There's a lot she could tell you, she knows more about some of our people than I do.'

'But she won't talk, Arthur,' Mum replied. 'Sometimes, I think she imagines she's white. She's ashamed of her family.'

'Aah, she's bin with whitefellas too long. They make her feel 'shamed, that's what white people do to you. Why should we be 'shamed, we bin here longer than them. You don't see the black man diggin' up the land, scarin' it. The white man got no sense.'

Arthur had land of his own, at Mukinbudin, and he kept a part of it uncleared so that the wildlife could prosper in peace.

I sat and listened to many conversations between Mum and Arthur.

Whenever he turned up for a visit Mum would ring me at home and say, 'He's here!' and I would go rushing over.

One afternoon, I wandered out to the backyard to find Nan and Arthur under a gum tree, jabbering away in what sounded to me like a foreign language. I sat down very quietly on the steps.

After a few minutes, Nan said, 'My eyes aren't that bad, Sally. I can see you there, spyin' on us.'

'I'm not spying,' I defended myself. 'Keep talking, don't let me stop you.'

'We're not talkin' no more,' Nan said.

I went inside. 'Mum,' I said excitedly, 'they were talking

15

in their own language!'

'What, Nanna too?'

'Yep! She was jabbering away as though she always talked like that. I wouldn't have thought she'd remember after all these years. It's a ray of hope, Mum. She could easily have forgotten it — a language needs to be used to be remembered. It must mean it was important to her. She might turn into a proud blackfella yet.'

Over the following weeks, whenever I saw Nan I'd bring up the topic of her language. She was very defensive at first, but she gradually came round. One day she said, 'Hey, Sally, you know what goombo is?'

I grinned. 'No, what?'

'Wee wee.' Nan chuckled and walked off.

She told me many words after that, but I could never get her to say a whole sentence for me. She was willing to give only a little.

I had married Paul Morgan in 1971, while I was still at University. Paul spent most of his childhood in the north-west of Western Australia — his parents were missionaries. When he was thirteen they had moved to Perth to start a hostel for mission children who came to the city to attend high school. At that time, Paul spoke only pidgin English; he'd had a hard time adjusting to his new life at first. Our daughter, Ambelin, was born in 1975 and our son Blaze in 1977. In 1975, after completing a post-graduate course in psychology, I gave up study for a while to concentrate on being a wife and mother. Now, four years later, I had more time to myself — and so I had made the big decision to write about our family.

2

AUNT JUDY

Mum took my ambition more seriously the following week when I bought a typewriter. As she watched my jerky two-finger typing effort she said, 'It'll take you a lifetime to do a page at that rate.'

'I'll get quicker. It's just practice.'

'What are you typing, anyway?'

'I'm putting down what I know. It's not much, but it's a start. Then I'm going to try to fill in what I don't know, and I expect you to help me.'

'I can't help you. I don't know anything.'

'You only *think* you don't know anything. I'm sure if you searched your mind you'd come up with something.'

'It's no use counting on me, Sally.'

'You're as bad as Nan sometimes! You've got to help me, you're my mother, it's your duty.'

'No need to be so dramatic. You know I'd help you if I could.'

'But you can help me, Mum. You've spent all your life with Nan. You must be able to tell me something about her. What seems unimportant to you could be a really good lead for me. For example, how come Nan and Aunty Judy are so close?'

I knew that Nan and Judy Drake-Brockman had been friends all their lives.

'I've told you before, Nan was Judy's nursemaid. Judy was quite sick as a child; I suppose that drew them closer together.'

'How come Nan was their nursemaid?'

'Nan came from the station that Judy's father owned. Corunna Downs, it was called.'

'You know,' I said slowly, 'I think I'll go and talk to Judy. I don't know why I didn't think of it before. There, you see, you've given me a lead already!'

'Judy won't tell you anything, she and Nan both love secrets. What are you going to ask her?'

'Oh, about the station and why they chose Nan to come down to Perth. I'll ask her about Ivanhoe, too.' Ivanhoe was the grand old house in Claremont, on the banks of the Swan River, where Nan had spent much of her working life. 'I went to Battye Library the other day, Mum,' I went on. 'It's a history library. Western Australian history. I wanted to read up about Aborigines.'

'Did you find out anything interesting?'

'I sure did. I found out there was a lot to be ashamed of.'

'You mean we should feel ashamed?'

'No, I mean Australia should.'

Mum sat down. 'Tell me.'

'Well, when Nan was younger, Aborigines were considered subnormal and not capable of being educated the way whites were. You know, the pastoral industry was built on the back of slave labour. Aboriginal people were forced to work; if they didn't, the station owners called the police in. I always thought Australia was different to America, Mum, but we had slavery here, too. The people may not have been sold on the blocks the way the American Negroes were, but they were owned, just the same.'

'I know,' Mum said. There were tears in her eyes. 'They were treated just awful. I know Nan...' She stopped.

'What were you going to say?'

'Nothing.'

'Yes, you were.'

'I don't want to talk about it now. Maybe later. If you want my help, you'll have to give me time.'

I could see Mum was quite upset. 'Okay, I'll give you all the time you want, as long as you help me.'

'I'll try.' She sighed. 'If you talk to Judy, it'll upset Nan. And when she finds out you want to write a book, she'll be *really* upset. Can't you just leave the past buried? It won't hurt anyone then.'

'Mum,' I reasoned, 'it's already hurt people. It's hurt you and me and Nan, all of us. I mean, for years, I've been telling people I'm Indian! I have a right to know my own history. Come to think of it, you've never told me why you lied to us about that.'

'I've had enough for one night.' Mum rose quickly to her feet. 'See Judy if you like, but don't upset Nan.'

I remembered something else. 'Hey, I meant to tell you, I got a copy of your birth certificate the other day.'

Mum sat down just as quickly. 'I didn't know you could do that.'

'It's easy. You just apply to the Registrar General's Office. I said I wanted it for the purposes of family history. I tried to get Nan's and Arthur's, but they didn't have them. Hardly any Aboriginal people had birth certificates in those days.'

'Sally...' Mum said tentatively, 'who did they say my father was? Was that on the certificate?'

'There was just a blank there, Mum. I'm sorry.'

'Just a blank,' Mum muttered slowly. 'That's awful. It's as though nobody owns me.'

I hadn't anticipated Mum being so cut up about it. I felt awful. She'd known all her life that Nan had never married.

'I'm really sorry, Mum,' I said gently. 'I got your certificate because I thought it might help me, but all it told me was that you were born in King Edward Memorial Hospital. I wouldn't have thought they'd have let Aboriginal women in there in those days.'

'Well, at least you've found out something, Sally.'

'You've asked Nan who your father was, haven't you?'

'Yes.'

'Maybe Judy would know.'

Mum sighed. 'She probably does, but she won't tell. I asked her once.'

'I bet you never asked her straight out. You beat around the bush too much. Why don't you corner her and say, "Judy, I want to know who my father is and I'm not leaving here till I find out"?'

Mum grinned. 'I couldn't do that, I'm not brave enough. Anyway, he couldn't have cared less about me or he would have contacted me. And when Nan needed help, there was no one. He can't be much of a man.'

'You know, Mum, just on a logical basis, it must be someone who mixed with the mob at Ivanhoe.'

'You reckon?'

'Yeah. It makes sense. Did any single blokes ever stay there?'

'No. Jack Grime lived there for years, but it wouldn't have been him.' Mum laughed. 'He was an English gentleman.'

A few days later, I rang Aunty Judy. I explained that I was writing a book about Nan and Arthur and thought she might be able to help me. We agreed that I would come down for lunch. She said she could tell me who Nan's father was. I was surprised. I had expected to encounter opposition. I felt really excited after our talk on the telephone. Would I really discover who my great-grandfather was? If I was lucky, I might even find out about my grandfather as well. I was so filled with optimism I leapt up and down three times and gave God the thumbs-up sign.

Mum agreed to drop me in Cottesloe, where Judy was now living, and mind the children while we had our talk.

'Can't I come, Mum?' Amber wailed as we pulled up out the front of Judy's house on the appointed day.

'Sorry, Amber,' I replied, 'this is private.' I leapt from the car. 'Wish me luck, Mum.'

During lunch, Aunty Judy said, 'You know, I think I have some old photos of your mother you'd be interested in.'

'Oh, great! I'd really appreciate that.'

'I'll tell you what I know about the station, but it's not a lot.'

After our meal, we retired to more comfortable chairs in the lounge-room.

'Now, dear,' Aunty Judy said, 'what would you like to know?'

'Well, first of all, I'd like to know who Nan's father was and also a bit about her life at Ivanhoe.'

'Well, that's no problem. My mother told me that Nan's father was a mystery man, a chap they called Maltese Sam. He used to be cook on Corunna Downs. He was supposed to have come from a wealthy Maltese family. My mother said that he always used to tell them that one day, he was going back to Malta to claim his inheritance. The trouble was, he was a drinker. He'd save money for the trip, then he'd go on a binge and have to start all over again. He used to talk to my father, Howden, a lot. He was proud Nanna was his little girl.'

'Did he ever visit Nan when she was at Ivanhoe?'

'Yes, I think he did, once. But he was drunk, and wanted to take Nanna away with him. Nan was frightened, she didn't want to go, so my mother said to him, "You go back to Malta and put things right. When you've claimed your inheritance, you can have Daisy." We never saw him again. Nan didn't want to go with him, we were her family by then. I was only a child, of course. My mother told me the story.'

'How old was Nan when she came down to Perth?'

'Fifteen or sixteen.'

'And what were her duties at Ivanhoe?'

'She looked after us children.'

'Aunty Judy, do you know who Mum's father is? Mum wants to know and Nan won't tell her. It's very important to her.'

'I'm not sure I should tell you.' Aunty Judy paused and looked at me silently for a few seconds. Then she said slowly: 'All right, everybody knows who her father was. It was Jack Grime. Everyone always said that Gladdie's the image of him. He was an Englishman, an engineer. A very clever man. He lived with us at Ivanhoe, he was a friend of my father's. He was very fond of your mother. When she was working as a florist, he'd call in to see her. We could always tell when he'd been to see Gladdie, he'd have a certain look on his face.'

'Did he ever marry and have other children?'

'No. He spent the rest of his life in Sydney. He was about eighty-six when he died.'

'That couldn't have been so long ago. If he was so fond of Mum, you'd think he'd have left her something in his will. Not necessarily money, just a token to say he owned her. After all, she was his only child.'

'No, there was nothing. He wasn't a wealthy man, there was no money to leave. You know Roberta?'

'Yes, Mum's been out to dinner with her a few times.'

'Well, she's the daughter of Jack's brother, Robert. She's Gladdie's first cousin.'

'Mum doesn't know that. Does Roberta?'

'Yes. She asked me a year ago whether she should say something to your mother. I said it'd be better to leave it.'

'Perhaps Mum could talk to her.'

'Yes, she could.'

'Can you tell me anything about Nan's mother?'

'Not a lot. Her name was Annie, she was a magnificent-looking woman. She was a good dressmaker — she could design anything.'

Our conversation continued for another half-hour or so. I kept thinking, did Mum really know who her father was? Was she really against me digging up the past, just like Nan? I had one last question.

'Aunty Judy, I was talking to Arthur, Nan's brother, the other day and he said that his father was the same as yours, Alfred Howden Drake-Brockman. Isn't it possible he could have been Nan's father as well?'

'No. I've told you what I know — who Nan's father is. I'm certain Arthur's father wasn't Howden. I don't know who his father was.'

'Arthur also told me about his half-brother, Albert. He

said Howden was his father too.'

'Well, he went by the name of Brockman, so I suppose it might be possible, but certainly not the other two. You know who you should talk to, don't you? Mum-mum. She's still alive, and better than she's been for a long time.' Mum-mum was a pet name for Aunty Judy's mother, Alice.

'She must be in her nineties by now,' I said. 'Do you think she'd mind talking to me?'

'I don't think so. She's in a nursing home in Wollongong. You could probably stay with June.' June was Judy's younger sister, Nan had been her nursemaid, too.

'I'll think about it, Aunty Judy. Thanks a lot.'

I walked out to the front gate. Just as I opened it, Mum pulled up in the car.

'How did you go?' she said eagerly.

'All right,' I replied. 'Mum, are you sure you don't know who your father is?'

Mum was immediately on the defensive. 'Of course I don't know who my father is, Sally. Didn't you find out, after all?' She was disappointed. I felt ashamed of myself for doubting her.

'I found out. It was Jack Grime, and Roberta is your first cousin.'

'Oh God, I can't believe it!' She was stunned.

'Can you remember anything about him, Mum? You're supposed to look a lot like him.'

'Only that he used to wear a big gold watch that chimed. I thought it was magical.'

'Judy said he used to visit you when you were working as a florist. Can you recall that?'

'Well yes, he popped in now and then, but a lot of people did. Sometimes, I would go and have lunch with him at Ivanhoe, after Nan had left there...To think I was lunching with my own father!'

An overwhelming sadness struck me. My mother was fifty-five and she'd only just discovered who her father was.

'Mum, are you going to say anything to Nan?'

'Not now, maybe later, after I've had time to think things

over. Don't you say anything, will you?'

'No. Does she know I've been to see Judy?'

'Yes. She's been in a bad mood all week. Did you find out anything else?'

'Judy says Nan's father was a bloke called Maltese Sam. That he came from a wealthy family and wanted to take Nan away with him.'

'Maltese Sam? I've never heard anyone talk about him. Arthur's coming tomorrow night, I'll ask him what he thinks. Of course, you know who he says is Nan's father, don't you?'

'Yeah. Judy doesn't agree with him.'

The following evening, after we'd finished tea, I turned to Arthur. 'I visited Judith Drake-Brockman the other day. I thought she might be able to tell me about Corunna Downs and something about Nan.'

'You wanna know about Corunna, you come to me. I knew all the people there.'

'I know you did.' I paused. 'Judy told me Nan's father was a chap by the name of Maltese Sam, have you ever heard of him?'

'She said *what*?'

I repeated my question.

'Don't you listen to her,' he said. 'She never lived on the station, how would she know?'

'Well, she got the story from her mother, Alice, who got it from her husband, Howden, who said Annie had confided in him.'

Arthur threw back his head and laughed. Then he thumped his fist on the arm of his chair and said, 'Now you listen to me, Daisy's father is the same as mine. Daisy is my only full sister. Albert, he's our half-brother, his father was Howden, too, but his mother was a different woman. Are you gunna take the word of white people against your own flesh and blood? I got no papers to prove what I'm sayin'. Nobody cared how many blackfellas were born in those days, nor how many died. I know because my mother, Annie, told me. She said Daisy and I belonged to one another.'

24

Arthur had us both nearly convinced, except for one thing: he avoided our eyes. Mum and I both knew there was something he wasn't telling us. 'You're sure about this, Arthur?' I asked him.

'Too right! Before Howden married his first wife, Nell, he owned us, we went by his name, but then he changed our names. He didn't want to own us no more. Alice was his second wife, of course.' Then he said, 'You know, if only you could get Daisy to talk, she could tell you so much.'

I sighed. 'She won't talk, Arthur. You know a lot about Nan, can't you tell us?'

He was silent for a moment, thoughtful. Then he said, 'I'd like to, I really would, but it'd be breakin' a trust. There's some things Daisy's got to tell herself. I can't say no more.'

After he left, Mum and I sat analysing everything for ages. We were confused. We knew that the small pieces of information we now possessed weren't the complete truth.

'Sally,' Mum said at last, 'I don't think we'll ever know the full story. I think we're going to have to be satisfied with guesses.' She sighed. 'Anyway, I've had enough for one night.'

3

PART OF OUR HISTORY

A few days later, I found myself alone with Nan. Mum had gone to the shops and would be back in a few minutes. I wasn't intending to say anything to Nan about my trip to Judy's, I wasn't in the mood for an argument. Uncharacteristically, she began following me around the house, and I suddenly realised she was anxious to hear what Judy had told me.

Finally, after half an hour of chatting about the weather and whatever came into her head, she blurted out: 'Well, what did she tell you?'

We went and sat down in the lounge-room. After we'd made ourselves comfortable, I said, 'Well, she told me that you were the nursemaid at Ivanhoe.'

Nan grunted. 'Hmmph, that and everything else.'

'You've always worked hard, haven't you, Nan?'

'Always, too hard.'

'Judy also said your father was a bloke called Maltese Sam.'

'What?' Nan looked astonished.

'She said your father was called Maltese Sam, and that he visited you at Ivanhoe and wanted to take you away with him. Do you remember anyone visiting you there?'

'Only Arthur, and that wasn't till I was older.'

'There was no one else, you're sure?'

'I'd know if I had visitors, wouldn't I? I'm not stupid, Sally, despite what you kids might think.'

'We don't think you're stupid.'

Nan pressed her lips together and stared hard at the red-brick fireplace.

'Nan,' I said gently, 'was your father Maltese Sam?'

She sighed, then murmured, 'Well, if Judy says he is, then I s'pose it's true.' I looked at her closely; there were tears in her eyes. I suddenly realised she was hurt, and I felt terrible, because I'd caused it. I began to talk about my children and the latest naughty things they'd been up to. We had a chuckle, and then I said, 'Would you have liked to have had more children, Nan?'

She shrugged her shoulders and looked away. 'Think I'll do some gardening now, Sal. Those leaves need raking up.'

She left me sitting alone and confused in the lounge-room. What was she hiding? Why couldn't she just be honest with us? Surely she realised we didn't blame her for anything. Surely she realised we loved her? I swallowed the lump that was rising in my throat. One thing I was sure of: before this was over, Mum and I would have shed more than our fair share of tears.

When Mum returned, she said, 'Have you spoken to Nan?'

'Yes, but only about Maltese Sam. I don't think she believes he was her father, but she won't say anything.'

'I tell you what, I'll get a few days off work and make a big fuss of her and then, when she's in a good mood, I'll ask her about it.'

Three evenings later, after they'd finished eating a big roast dinner, Mum said quietly, 'Don't go and watch television yet, Nan, I want to talk to you. Sit with me for a while.'

'I'm not talking about the past, Gladdie. It makes me sick to talk about the past.'

'I'm only going to ask you one question. Then you can do whatever you like, all right?' Nan sat still. 'Now, you know

Sally's trying to write a book about the family?'

'Yes. I don't know why she wants to tell everyone our business.'

'Why shouldn't she write a book?' Mum said firmly. 'There's been nothing written about people like us, all the history's about the white man. There's nothing about Aboriginal people and what they've been through.'

'All right,' she muttered, 'what do you want to ask?'

'When you write a book, it has to be the truth. You can't put lies in a book. You know that, don't you Nan?'

Nan nodded.

'Good. Now, I want to know who you think your father was. Judy says it was Maltese Sam and Arthur says it was Howden. Well, I'm not interested in what they say. I want to know what *you* say. Nan, who do you think he really was?'

Nan was quiet for a few seconds and then, pressing her lips together, she said very slowly, 'I...think...my father was...Howden Drake-Brockman.'

It was a small victory, but an important one. Not so much for the knowledge, but for the fact that Nan had finally found it possible to trust her family with a piece of information that was important to her.

Mum gave Nan a week to recover before tackling her about Jack Grime. She'd been spending more time at home and, in a gentle way, talking about the past.

Finally one evening, she said, 'Nan, I know who my father was.' Nan was silent. 'It was Jack Grime, wasn't it?' Silence. 'Wasn't it, Nan?'

'Judy tell you that, did she?'

'Yes.'

'Well, if that's what she says.'

'But was he, Nan?'

'I did love Jack.'

'What happened, then? Why didn't it work out?'

'How could it? He was well-off, high society. He mixed with all the wealthy white people, I was just a black servant.'

She ignored Mum's pleas to tell her more and disappeared into her room, leaving Mum to cry on her own.

When Mum and I talked about this later, Mum said, 'You know, Jack Grime probably was my father. If he was, I feel very bitter towards him. There was never any acknowledgement or feeling of love from him. I was just one of the kids. Later, when he moved east with Judy's family, he never wrote, there were no goodbyes, I never saw or heard from him again. All I can remember is that he used to tell wonderful stories. He was like an uncle, but definitely not a father.'

We hoped that Nan would tell us more about the past, especially about the people she had known on Corunna Downs. Mum was anxious to hear about Annie, her grandmother, and her great-grandmother, and I was keen to learn what life had been like for the people in those days. To our great disappointment, Nan would tell us nothing. She maintained that if we wanted to find out about the past, we must do it without her help. 'I'm taking my secrets to the grave,' she said dramatically one day.

Over the next few years, Arthur continued to visit regularly and to talk in snatches about Corunna. Sometimes he'd say to Nan, 'Daisy, come and sit down. Tell your daughter and granddaughter about the past, tell them what they want to know.'

But Nan would not co-operate. She insisted that the things she knew were secrets, not to be shared with others. Arthur always countered this with, 'It's history, that's what it is. We're talkin' history. You could be talkin' it, too, but then, I s'pose you don't know what it is.'

Nan hated Arthur hinting that she might be ignorant. 'You always makin' out you're better than anyone else,' she told him. 'Well, you're not! You're just a stupid old black-fella, that's you!'

Arthur was incensed. Raising his voice, he said, 'You're a great one to talk. Here I am in my nineties and I can read the paper and write my own name, too. I been educated! I'm not like you, you're just ignorant!'

Nan was mortally offended. For a few seconds she was lost

for words, then she shouted, 'I don't know why I bother with you! You're always picking fights. You know they were s'posed to send me to school. It's not my fault I can't read or write. It hasn't done nothin' for you, anyway. I been listenin' to you, you can't even make up a good story!'

When Mum had finished waving goodbye to Arthur, she went in search of Nan. 'I'm fed up,' she said crossly. 'You're the one that picks the fights. He's your own brother.'

'He shouldn't have said that to me,' Nan replied in a grumbly sort of way. 'I can't help it if I can't read or write.' She looked sad and Mum was lost for words. It wasn't until then that she'd realised how deeply Nan felt about the whole thing.

'Lots of people can't read or write,' Mum said gently, 'white people, too. It doesn't make you any better than anyone else.'

'Yes, it does,' Nan muttered, 'I always wanted to learn. Oh, go away, Gladdie, leave me in peace.'

We all avoided mentioning anything to do with reading or writing after that; we didn't want Nan to think we were looking down on her.

The next time I saw Arthur, he asked me to tell him about the book I was writing.

'I want to write the history of my own family,' I told him.
'Why?'

'Well, there's almost nothing written from a personal point of view about Aboriginal people. All our history is about the white man. No one knows what it was like for us. A lot of our history has been lost, people have been too frightened to say anything. There's a good deal of it we can't even get at, Arthur. There are files about Aboriginals that go way back, and the government won't release them. You take the old police files, they're not even held by Battye Library, they're controlled by the police. And they don't like letting them out, because there are so many instances of police abusing their power when they were supposed to be Protectors of Aborigines that it's not funny! Our government had terrible policies for Aboriginal people. Thousands of families in Australia were destroyed by the government policy of taking children away. None of that happened to white people. I know Nan doesn't agree with what I'm doing. She thinks I'm trying to make trouble, but I'm not. I just want to try to tell a little bit of the other side of the story.'

Arthur was silent for a few seconds, then he said thoughtfully, 'Daisy doesn't agree, I know that. I think she's been brainwashed. I tell you how I look at it: it's part of our history, like you say. And everyone's interested in history. Do you think you could put my story in that book of yours?'

'Oh Arthur, I'd love to!'

'Then we got a deal. You got that tape recorder of yours? We'll use that. You just listen to what I got to say, and if you want to ask questions, you stop me. Some things I might tell you, I don't want in the book, is that all right?'

'I won't put anything in you don't want me to.'

It took three months or more to record Arthur's story. We went over and over the same incidents, and each time he added a little more detail. He had a fantastic memory. Sometimes, when he spoke, it was as if he was actually reliving what had happened. We became very close. There were times when I worried that I was working him too hard, but if I slacked off, he'd say: 'We haven't finished yet, you know.' He was always worried about my cassette recorder. I had to check it each time to make sure it was working. 'You don't want to miss nothin',' he'd remind me.

One evening, after I'd spent a long session with Arthur, I fell into bed exhausted. That night, I had a dream. I knew he was going to die.

'What's wrong?' Paul asked me the following morning when I burst into tears over my cornflakes.

'It's Arthur,' I sobbed, 'he's going to die.'

'Aw, Sal,' Paul said, 'what makes you think something like that.'

'I dreamt about it last night.'

'Just because he's old doesn't mean he's about to die.'

'He is. I know he is. And I think he knows he's going, that's

31

why he wants to get his story done.'

'Well, if he is, there's nothing you can do about it. The best thing is to finish his story, seeing it means so much to him.'

Later that day, I rang Mum.

'Mum, it's about Arthur...I don't know how to say this.'

'What's wrong?'

'I had a dream last night. He's going to die soon. We've got to get his story finished.'

'Oh Sally, Arthur's not going to die, the doctors have only just given him a clean bill of health.'

'No Mum, I'm very sure about this.'

'Are you sure your dream wasn't about Nan? She's the one that hasn't been feeling well.'

'No, Mum. It's the old boy. And you know how keen he is about his story. We've got to drop everything and spend as much time as we can with him. Paul said he'll mind the kids. You'll have to take me over to see him.'

'I wish you'd got your licence when you were younger.'

'I'll get it one day. Anyway, it gives you something to do. Your life would be dull without me, Mum.'

'I suppose you're right. Sally...do you think he knows?'

'Yes. You watch his face the next time he talks, there's a sort of glow about it, as though he can see something we can't. A glimpse of heaven, maybe. As though he's not really here any more.'

'It's funny you saying that. I noticed the other night he was different. He's still the same old Arthur, but changed somehow.'

'Yeah...' I could tell by the tone of Mum's voice that if we pursued this conversation any further, we'd both start crying.

So it was that I spent the next few weeks non-stop recording everything I could. When we finished, we were both pleased.

'We've done it,' Arthur laughed. 'We've done it! I got no more story to tell now.'

'I can't believe it,' I said. 'We've actually finished.'

'I got a good story, eh?'

'You sure have.'

'You think people will read that?'

'Of course they will, and they'll love it. If they don't, they've got no heart.'

'Now, if only you could get Daisy to talk.'

'I don't think she ever will, Arthur.'

'Aah, she's too set in her ways. She's funny about secrets. She doesn't understand history.'

'Yeah, well, I'll keep hoping.'

'What you gunna do now, you gunna type that all up?'

'Yep. I'll finish typing all the cassettes. Then I'll put it all together — we've got bits and pieces all over the place.'

'I been wantin' to get this done all my life. Different people, they say, "Arthur, we'll write your story", but none of them come back to see me. I'm better off without them. It's better your own flesh and blood writes something like that.'

'I think you're right. You know I'm going to Sydney, don't you?'

'I heard about that. What you goin' over there for?'

'I want to meet Alice Drake-Brockman. I thought I'd ask her about the old days, and who Mum's father is.'

'Say hello to her for me.'

'I will. I'm only going for a week. When I get back, we can talk some more.'

'Too right. 'Cause you know I'm going back to Mucka, don't you?'

'No. I thought you were going to stay in Perth a bit longer.'

'I got a yearning for that place. My own home, my land. I been away too long. Can you understand that?'

'Yes.'

'Anyway, I told you my story now. You'll look after it, won't you?'

'Yes, of course I will.' I couldn't say any more. I had a lump in my throat. I knew he wanted to die on his own land.

4

LINKS WITH THE PAST

'Are you sure it's wise, going to Sydney now, Sal? Why don't you wait till after the baby's born?' It was now 1982 and I was expecting my third child.

'It's too important to wait, Mum. Alice is in her nineties. How do I know she'll be alive in three months' time?'

The following week, I flew to Sydney, then caught the bus to Wollongong. Aunty June, Judy's sister, and her husband, Angus, met me at the bus station. I felt very nervous. The last time I'd seen them I was a child; now I was a woman with a mission.

I could not have had two kinder hosts. They did everything to make me feel at home. We swapped many funny yarns and stories about home.

Alice Drake-Brockman was in a nearby nursing home. She was ninety-three and in the best of health. Aunty June took me to the home and explained who I was and why I was there.

'You look a lot like your mother,' Alice said. 'Now, tell me, how is Daisy?'

'She's fine — getting old, though. Her eyesight isn't too good.'

'It's been years since I've seen her.'

'I know.'

'So you want to know a bit about Corunna, eh?'

'Would you mind if I asked you a few questions?'

'Go ahead.'

'Can you tell me who Nan's father might have been, Alice?'

'Your great-grandfather was a Maltese, I think he came from a wealthy family, but was the younger son. He was always saying he must go back and right his affairs in the old country, but he never got past the nearest pub. One time, I think he managed to get as far as Carnarvon, then he spent all his money and had to come back again.'

'Did you ever meet Nan's mother?'

'Oh yes! She was a born designer. On the hard ground she'd cut out dresses, leg-o'-mutton sleeves and all. She could design anything. I didn't get to know her well, because I left the station, and when I left, I took Daisy with me. Annie said to me, "Take her with you, mistress. I don't want my daughter to grow up and marry a native, take her with you." It was at her request that I took Daisy. Of course, what I was doing was illegal, you weren't supposed to bring natives into Perth. The magistrate said, "I can't give you permission to take her, because that's against the law, but the captain can't refuse her passage." Daisy was fourteen when she came with me and terrified of the sea. She'd never even seen a boat, living inland all those years. I became a well-known authority on native affairs after that. I was quoted in the *Herald*. I said, "Make a test case out of me." When I was prosecuted, they said, "How do you plead, guilty or not guilty?" My husband stood up and said, "Guilty, M'Lord." They asked us our reasons and I told them her own mother had said, "Don't leave my daughter here, take her with you." I brought other native girls in after that. I'd train them, then find friends who wanted maids.'

'What was Corunna Downs Station like then?'

'I can't tell you a lot about that, because I was only there once. After my husband sold Corunna, he bought Towera, about nine hundred miles away. When my husband was on Corunna, all the squatters were asked to send boys down to school — I suppose that was when Albert and Arthur went down. Albert came back to work at Corunna. But Arthur ran away. He had ambitions of his own.' She paused. 'Corunna Downs was named by my husband. There's a poem, *Corunna*. He was reading a book at the time with the natives, and the poem was in it. So that's what he named the station. When I went to Corunna, there were about forty natives working for us. Every Sunday night, we'd roll the piano out onto the verandah. It'd be cold, so we'd have a big log fire out in the open. The natives would sit around and we'd have a church service and a sing-song. The natives just loved it. At nine o'clock, we'd stop. Then they'd all be given cocoa and hot buns. That was their life. The natives never liked to work. You had to work with them if you wanted them to work. They always wanted to go walkabout. They couldn't stand the tedium of the same job. We used to change their jobs. Daisy always had that tendency. She'd get tired of one job, so I'd say, "Come on, let's chuck the housework" and we'd go shopping.'

'Did Nan ever see her mother again?'

'Yes. I sent her back with Howden for a holiday. I said, "Take her back, let her see her mother." She saw them and she was happy, but by then, we'd become her family.'

'What were her duties at Ivanhoe?'

'Oh, housework, that sort of thing. She was always good with Granny, too. She'd come quietly and take her shoes off after lunch when it was time for her to have her afternoon sleep. She was simply devoted. No white trained nurse had better experience. She grew up loving us and we were her family — there were no servants. It was just family life. She couldn't read a clock, but she knew the time better than any of us. She knew everybody's handwriting that came to that place.'

'Why did she leave Ivanhoe?'

'The police came and took Daisy from me. She was man-powered during the war. No one could have home-help. She was a wonderful cook. Later, she rented a little house near the Ocean Beach Hotel. I gave her quite a lot of furniture.'

'Can you tell me who my mother's father might have been?'

'No, I couldn't tell you. He must have been white, maybe a station hand. I had no idea Daisy was having a baby. My husband said to me one night, "I think you'd better get up, Daisy seems to be in pain." She slept in a room just off ours. She was groaning and I said, "What's up, Daisy?" She said, "I don't know, mistress, but I think I'm going to have a baby." I hadn't any idea — she always wore loose dresses. So I went and packed a suitcase and took her to the hospital. The baby was born a few hours later, but who the father was, we never found out.

'Gladys was always a beautiful girl. She went to Parkerville — we took her there. That was a home run by the Church of England sisters, a charity home for orphans. She grew up with just as nice manners as anybody could wish. Later, when she was grown up, I said to the florist in Claremont, "Will you take this girl?" They said, "No, we can't take a native, you know it's forbidden." I said, "Will you take her on trial for me? I just can't bear to think of her becoming a servant somewhere." So they took her on trial to please me, and they kept her as one of the family. She was like a lovely Grecian girl. She never looked back. She was so well brought up by those Church of England sisters.'

When Alice finished talking, I felt a little stunned. All my life, I'd been under the impression that Mum had lived with Nan at Ivanhoe. It was a shock to discover that she'd been placed in a children's home. Why hadn't she told us?

'Well, it's been very interesting talking to you.' I smiled. 'I've heard so much about you over the years. May I come and see you again?'

'Any time you like, dear.'

I spoke with Alice again after that, and she told me a little more about Corunna and the early days. I was pleased I'd made the trip, even though I hadn't come up with a great deal of new information.

In talking to Alice, it dawned on me how different Australian society must have been in those days. There would have been a strong English tradition amongst the upper classes. I could understand the effects these attitudes could have had on someone like Nan. She must have felt terribly out of place. At the same time I was aware that it would be unfair of me to judge Alice's attitudes from my standpoint in the 1980s.

On my return from Sydney, Mum met me at the airport. 'What did you find out?' was her first eager question.

'Quite a lot,' I replied. 'I'm really glad I went. Nothing startling, but I think sometimes you learn more from what people don't tell you than from what they do.'

On the way home in the car, I described my trip in detail to Mum. But I didn't mention Parkerville Children's Home. I wasn't sure how to tackle her about that.

The following day, I left with Paul and the children to spend two weeks at Lancelin, a small fishing town north of Perth. It was the first real holiday we'd had for a long time. When I returned to Perth, I felt refreshed and ready to tackle Mum.

On my first day back, I popped round to visit my sister Jill. Jill was living in Subiaco, sharing a house with Helen, our youngest sister. I was quietly sipping a cup of coffee when she suddenly said, 'Oh goodness, I forgot! You don't know, do you?'

'Know what?'

She shrugged her shoulders in a helpless kind of way. 'Arthur,' she said. 'He's dead. He died a few days ago. He went home to Mukinbudin and apparently he had a heart attack and died virtually straight away.'

I wanted to cry, but I couldn't. I felt too shocked. I knew he wanted to go, but the reality of never being able to talk to him again was very painful. He was one of the few links I had with the past.

I saw Mum that afternoon. 'You've heard about Arthur, haven't you?' she said.

I nodded. 'Did you see him before he went to Mucka?'

'Yes. I think he came round to say goodbye. He knew he was going to die once he got to Mucka, he wanted to see us all one last time. He really wanted to see you, Sally.'

I went to Arthur's funeral with my brother Bill and Mum. I couldn't feel sad for him any more. I knew he was tired of this life, and I knew he was happy. When we got home, we described the funeral to Nan. She hadn't wanted to go. She had a good cry, then she said, 'Well, I can't be too sad for him, he wanted to go. I got no brother now.' After that, she rarely mentioned him.

About a week after Arthur's funeral I decided to tackle Mum about Parkerville Children's Home. She had never told any of us she'd been brought up in a home. She'd always led us to believe that she had spent all her childhood at Ivanhoe.

I popped the question over afternoon tea. Mum was shocked. Before she had time to gather her wits, I said, 'You deliberately misled us. All these years I thought you were brought up at Ivanhoe with Judy and June. Why on earth didn't you tell us the truth?'

'You're making a big deal out of nothing,' she replied. 'I spent holidays at Ivanhoe. Anyway, there's nothing to tell.'

'Oh, come on, Mum, this is me you're talking to, not some stranger off the street! You think I can't tell when you're hiding things? I know you too well. I want you to tell me what it was like.'

'I told you before, Sally,' she said in a very annoyed way, 'there's nothing to tell. Who told you I was brought up in Parkerville, anyway?'

'Alice. How did you think I felt, finding out like that? I was shocked. You're supposed to be helping me with this book and here you are, hoarding your own little secrets. And you complain about Nan!'

'All right, all right! I'll tell you about it, one day.'

I spent the next few months transcribing Arthur's cassettes and putting his story together. It was very important to me to finish his story. I owed him a great debt. He'd told me so much about himself and his life, and, in doing so, he'd told me something about my own heritage.

When I had completed it all, I rang Mum.

'It's finished,' I told her when she answered the phone.

'What's finished?'

'Arthur's story.'

'Can I come and read it?'

'That's what I'm ringing you for.'

5

ARTHUR CORUNNA'S STORY

(c. 1893 – c. 1950)

Corunna Downs

My name is Arthur Corunna. I can't tell you how old I am exactly, because I don't know. A few years ago, I wrote to Alice Drake-Brockman, my father's second wife, and asked her if she knew my age. She said that I could have been born around 1893 or 1894. Later, her daughter Judy wrote to me and said I could have been born before that. So I guess I have to settle for around there somewhere. Anyway, I'm old, and proud of it.

The early years of my life were spent on Corunna Downs Station in the Pilbara, in the north of Western Australia. We called the top half of the station, where I lived, Mool-nya-moonya. The lower half, the outstation, we called Boog-gi-gee-moonya. The land of my people was all round there, from the Condin River to Nullagine, right through the Kimberleys.

After my people had worked for so long on the station, they were allowed to go walkabout. We would go for weeks at a time, from one station to another, visiting people that belonged to us. The eastern part of Western Australia, that's different. We call that Pukara. Our land was Yabara, the north.

My mother's name was Annie Padewani and my father was Alfred Howden Drake-Brockman, the white station-owner. We called him Good-da-goonya. He lived on Corunna Downs nine years before marrying his first wife, Eleanor Boddington. While on the station, he shared my Aboriginal father's two wives, Annie and Ginnie.

Ginnie, or Binddiding as we called her, was a big woman. She bossed my mother around. I used to cry for my mother when she was in a fight. I'd run round and grab her skirts and try and protect her from Ginnie. Ginnie only had one child by Howden: my half-brother, Albert.

My mother was small and pretty. She was very young when she had me. I was her first child. Then she had Lily by my Aboriginal father. Later, there was Daisy. She is my only sister who shares with me the same parents. I was a good deal older than her.

My Aboriginal father was one of the headmen of our tribe. He was a leader. He got our people to work on the station and, in return, he was given a rifle, tea, tobacco and sugar. He was a tall, powerful man. Many people were scared of him. Sometimes he would go walkabout, right down to Fremantle, then up through Leonora, Ethel Creek and back to Corunna Downs. Men were frightened of him because he was a boolyah man*.

My uncle and grandfather were also boolyah men. For centuries, the men in my family have been boolyah men. I remember when my grandfather was dying, he called me to him. I was only a kid. He said, 'You know I can't use my power to heal myself. I will pass my power into you and then I want you to heal me.' He did this, and I ran away and played, even though he was calling me. I was only a kid, I didn't understand. My grandfather died. It wasn't until years later

* *Boolyah man*—person who has attained a high degree of knowledge and who has special perceptive and combative skills. Also more commonly known as a *Maban*.

that I began to learn just what power he had given me.

One day, my Uncle Gibbya said to my mother, 'Never worry about Jilly-yung. (That was my Aboriginal name.) Never worry about him, I will look after him when I'm dead. I will always be close to him. He may not know I am there, I may be a bird in the tree or a lizard on the ground, but I will be close to him.' Uncle Gibbya was married to Annie's sister.

My Uncle Gibbya was a powerful rainmaker. He didn't always live on Corunna Downs. One day when he was visiting our people, Howden said to him, 'You can work with me on the station as long as you can make it rain.' My Uncle Gibbya said, 'I will make it rain. Three o'clock this afternoon, it will rain.' Howden looked at the sky. It was blue and cloudless. He shook his head. Later that day, white clouds began to gather, like a mob of sheep slowly coming in. At three o'clock, it rained. My uncle got his job. He was the best rainmaker in the area.

On the station, I wasn't called Arthur. I had my Aboriginal name, Jilly-yung, which meant 'silly young kid'. When I was a child, I copied everything everyone said. Repeated it like a ninety-nine parrot. The people would say, 'Silly young kid! Jilly-yung!'

I loved my mother, she was my favourite. My mother was always good to me. When others were against me, she stood by me. She used to tell me a story about a big snake. A snake especially for me, with pretty eggs. 'One day,' she said, 'you will be able to go and get these eggs.' I belonged to the snake, and I was anxious to see the pretty snake's eggs, but they took me away to the mission, and that finished that. It was a great mystery. If I had've stayed there, I would have gone through the Law, then I would've known. I didn't want to go through the Law. I was scared.

When we went on holidays, we called it going pink-eye. My Aboriginal father carried me on his shoulders when I was tired. I remember one time, it was at night and very dark, we were going through a gorge, when the feather foots*, ginnawandas, began to whistle. I was scared. The whistling means they want you to talk. They began lighting fires all along the gorge. After we called out our names, my family was allowed through.

One day, I took a tomato from the vegetable garden. I'd been watching it for days. Watching it grow big and round and red. Then I picked it and Dudley saw me. He was Howden Drake-Brockman's brother — we called him Irrabindi. He gave orders for my Aboriginal father to beat me.

I was beaten with a stirrup strap. I spun round and round, crying and crying. I was only a kid in a shirt in those days. My Aboriginal father never hit me unless an order was given. Then he had to do it, boss's orders. He was good to me otherwise, so I never kept any bad feelings against him.

Dudley Drake-Brockman wasn't like Howden. They were brothers, but they were different. Dudley was cruel and didn't like blackfellas. My people used to say about Dudley 'ngulloo-moolo', which means make him sick. We didn't want him there. In the end, he got sick and died.

I used to play with Pixie, Dudley's son. We used to fight, too, but I never beat him. I was afraid of his father. My mother used to say to me, 'Jilly-yung, never beat Pixie in a fight. When he wants to fight, you walk away.' She was a wise woman.

Howden was a good-looking man, well liked. He could ride all the horses there, even the buck jumpers. There was one big, black horse he named Corunna. He would always ride him when he went out baiting dingoes.

I remember the big dining-room, and a great, huge fan that we had to pull to cool people off who were eating there. They gave us a handful of raisins for doing that.

We had other jobs on the station besides pulling the fan. For every tin full of locusts we killed, we got one boiled lolly. I remember once, I was a tar boy for the shearers. In those days, it was blade shearing, not like the machines they have

---

* *feather foot (Ginnawandas)*—similar to the *Boolyah* or *Maban*. Person with special (magic) powers, often used for purposes of retribution. Similar also to *kadaicha man*.

now. The shed was stinking hot and the click, click, click of the shears made a rhythmic sound. I couldn't help goin' to sleep. Next thing I knew, I got a smack in the face. They were all singin' out 'TAR! TAR!' and I was asleep. When the girls brought down the dishes of cakes and buckets of tea, I made sure I was awake. I wasn't going to sleep through that.

I spent a lot of my time on the station with my brother, Albert, and my sister, Lily. When we were kids, we'd run round finding lizards, sticking our fingers in holes in the ground and wood. One time I did that, it was a snake. A snake won't chase you to bite and kill you. They just want to get away. You only get bitten if you tread on them, they're just protectin' themselves. People always try to kill snakes whenever they see them. They should leave them alone. You point a gun at a snake and he'll get goin', he knows what you goin' to do.

Albert was older than me and they started educatin' him early. Mrs McGregor was the teacher. Her husband worked on the station. She trained Albert to write on a slate with chalk. He had to speak English and learn the white man's ways and table manners. The other children weren't taught, only Albert and, later, me. She also gave us what you call religious instruction. We learnt all about the saints.

I went with my mother everywhere until they rounded me up to be educated. When I heard they were after me, I ran away. I didn't want to be educated. Also, I thought they wouldn't give me any meat at night-time. They caught me in the end, put me with Albert and Mrs McGregor. I wasn't allowed to talk blackfella after that. I liked my language, but I got a good hiding if I spoke it. I had to talk English. When I was sleeping on the homestead verandah, I used to call to my mother in my own language, 'Save me meat!'

Of course, when they caught me, Albert could already talk English. He used to study at the cook's table. One night, the cook was a bit late with our supper. Albert said, 'Go tell him.'

'Tell him what?' I said.

'Tell him to hurry up with the tucker.'

'Give me hurry up tea!' I shouted. I should have said, 'Hurry up and give me tea!' but I didn't know. Anyhow, the old cook came down and chased me round and round the kitchen. I was gone through the door with the cook chasin' after me! He never caught me, I was too quick. That was Albert. He was always puttin' things into my head, but he never did anythin' wrong himself.

Albert lost two fingers because of me. I chopped them off in the tank machine. He stuck his fingers in to try to stop the cogs going round. I turned the handle and chopped them off. We were just messing around, I didn't know he had his fingers in there. They used that machine to make tanks. You put in a straight bit of iron and bend it to make a boomerang circle. You only need three or four sheets to make a tank.

Even though Albert was the older one, I took no notice of him. I was the mischievous one. He was too frightened to do anything, sometimes he needed protecting.

I knew all the people on the station, they was a good mob. There was Chook Eye, Wongyung and Mingibung. They were housegirls. They used to take in cups of tea and look after the house. Then there was Tiger Minnie, she used to help Howden bait the dingoes. No one could bait like her. And Sarah, she was a big woman, she helped look after the garden. She grew pumpkins and cabbages for the cook and shooed the birds away. She was a half-caste, like me. When her own baby was born, it was nearly white. A white black-fella. We all reckoned those extra babies belonged either to old Fred Stream, or Sam Moody, the cook.

We used to call Sam Moody backwards, Moody Sam. He was a white man and a good cook. He'd bake bread, cut it in big slices and give it to the natives through the small kitchen window. He cooked meat, too. We'd all get bread and slices of meat. We'd poke our billies through that little window and get tea, too. If Moody Sam didn't cook, we'd get slices of mutton, make a fire outside and cook it ourselves. For extra meat, my people used to catch kangaroos and wild turkeys and fish from the creek. We'd go down to the creek and stand with our legs bent and apart, then we'd catch them between our knees. We'd grab them with our hands and throw them on the bank.

Old Fred Stream used to take me on trips to Condin. Corunna Downs wool used to be stored there, ready to be loaded on the sailing ships bound for Fremantle. Now they have a railway to Port Hedland. The stores were great big sheds and they housed goods as well as wool. One time, Fred Stream told me there were two saddles to be picked up, one for me and one for Albert. When they pulled them out, the rats had chewed away the straps.

On the way back to Corunna Downs, we camped at DeGrey Station. You should have seen all the pretty dresses come runnin' to meet our wagon. There was red, pink and green, all the colours of the rainbow. They was all runnin' to come and see me, too. I was only a little fella, I wasn't much in those days.

Some of the people there had pet pigs. They sold two to Fred Stream. Before we reached Corunna Downs, he knocked one on the head and cooked it in the ashes. I reckoned he was cruel, to eat a little pig like that! I couldn't look at him and I couldn't eat it. I kept thinking, fancy killing such a little pig. He was only a baby.

The next day, we came to a freshwater well and stopped to water the team. There were goats runnin' all over the place. Fred Stream watched all these goats, then he said, 'You want a goat?' I said, 'NO!' I didn't want him to catch and kill no baby goat. Anyhow, he rounded up a kid and a billy and when we got to Corunna Downs, we let them go. I don't know what happened to them. I couldn't take a little baby goat away from his mother. I'm tender-hearted, I don't believe in stealing anything from its mother.

I remember one time when I was very small there was so much food on the table on the verandah. I kept thinking to myself, I should eat more, I should finish it off. I knew I wasn't goin' to see food like that again for a long time. I just kept lookin' at all that food, thinkin' what a shame it was to go away and leave it. Even though my belly was already aching, I made myself eat more. A while later, I brought it all up. It must have been Christmas, because I was all dressed up in a shirt and pants that day.

There were always corroborees at Corunna. You needed special permission to watch them. We used to go with Howden. I hadn't been put through the Law by then, because I was still too young. That happens when you are fourteen or fifteen. I didn't want to go through the Law. I used to say, 'Don't let them do that to me, Mum.' I didn't want to be cut this way and that. For the real black ones, it was compulsory. I was half-caste, so I could be exempted. The women were just marked on the chest. Just one mark, here in the middle. That was their ceremony.

In those days, the women were given to you when you were only a baby. They had Old Dinah picked out for me. She used to help in the garden. She's dead and gone now, probably still waitin' for me in heaven. She was old enough to be my mother. I suppose, later, I could have had Helen Bunda for my wife. She was half-caste, too. Her mother was Nellie, or Moodgjera. Her father was a bullock driver.

There was wonderful wildlife on Corunna Downs. There was one little bird, he was a jay or a squeaker, he'd sing out three times and then the rains would come. He was never wrong. While he was there, there was always a good feed, but when he was gone, drought! When the little frogs sang out, we knew it was going to rain. They were lovely colours, white and brown with black spots. They were all different, there wasn't one the same. They used to get into the cooler and we'd have to clean it out. There were no insecticides then to kill the birds. That's why the blackfellas want their own land, with no white man messin' about destroyin' it.

All the people round there, we all belonged to each other. We were the tribe that made the station. The Drake-Brockmans didn't make it on their own. There were only a few white men there, ones that fixed the pumps and sank wells by contract. The blackfellas did the rest.

I remember seein' native people all chained up around the neck and hands, walkin' behind a policeman. They often passed the station that way. I used to think, what have they done to be treated like that? Made me want to cry, just watchin'. Sometimes, we'd hear about white men goin' shooting blackfellas for sport, just like we was some kind of animal. We'd all get scared, then. We didn't want that to happen to us. Aah, things was hard for the blackfellas in those days.

One day, I'd like to go back to Corunna Downs, see what improvements there are. I believe it was used for a military base during the war. When I was there, Brockmans built a hump and stuck a flagpole in it. Whenever any visitors came, they raised the Union Jack.

Aah, I always wish I'd never left there. It was my home. Sometimes, I wish I'd been born black as the ace of spades, then they'd never have took me. They only took half-castes. They took Albert and they took me and Katie, our friend. She was put in Parkerville. She had a big doll with her when she went. Others went, too. I was about eleven or twelve.

When I left, Lily cried and cried. She was only little, but she ran away and hid, no one could find her. I was her favourite. She was full-blood, real black, so they didn't want to take her. Daisy was only a baby, she didn't know what was goin' on.

They told my mother and the others we'd be back soon. We wouldn't be gone for long, they said. People were callin', 'Bring us back a shirt, bring us this, bring us that.' They didn't realise they wouldn't be seein' us no more. I thought they wanted us educated so we could help run the station some day. I was wrong.

When they came to get me, I clung to my mother and tried to sing* them. I wanted them to die. I was too young, I didn't know how to sing them properly. I cried and cried, calling to my mother, 'I don't want to go, I don't want to go!' I loved

---

* *sing* —to sing an incantation which is believed to have the power to kill the person against whom it is directed.

49

her. I called, 'I want to stop with you, I want to stop with you!'
I never saw her again.

The Mission

When we left Corunna Downs for the Swan Native and Half-Caste Mission, we had to travel through Marble Bar and then to Port Hedland. We caught the ship, the *Ballara*, me, my brother Albert, Pixie and Dudley Drake-Brockman. Albert and I travelled steerage. Sometimes, I'd sneak out and head towards the front end of the boat to see what was going on. Dudley Drake-Brockman would always catch me and shout, 'Get back to where you belong!'

It was a fine day when we arrived in Fremantle. We were taken straight to the mission, near the banks of the Swan River in Guildford.

The first thing they did was christen us. Canon Burton and Sophie McKintosh, I think she was the matron, were our godparents. We were christened 'Corunna', they didn't give us our father's name. That's when I got the name of Arthur, too. Albert had always been called Albert.

For a long time, I was very worried about my mother. She had always been good to me. She loved me. Albert didn't seem to mind so much, I think he was too frightened to mind anything. You see, we couldn't understand why they'd taken us away. We weren't their family. The mission wasn't anyone's family. They called us inmates, all us kids, we were all inmates, just like a prison.

We soon found out there were bullies at the mission. I suppose you get them everywhere. There was one that wanted to try us out. I was worried about Albert, I knew he couldn't fight his way out of a paper bag. He was bigger than me, older than me, yet I knew they could belt him up and tie him in knots. I had to take his part. I'd tackle whoever was beating up Albert and finish them off. They never tackled me again and they learnt not to touch Albert, because he was my brother. There was one bully there, he had everyone bluffed except me. He'd throw stones at me, call me names, but he'd never tackle me. When it came to knuckles, I got my fist in first.

I was different to Albert. I was made different. I could fall off a horse, do anything and there was never nothing damaged or broken, even if I landed on a rock. I'm like rubber, you can bounce me anywhere. Albert wasn't like that. He used to get sick a lot. I cried for him when he was sick. He was my brother.

One man that worked on the mission, Mr Ferguson, said about Albert and me, 'These boys have been well brought up. They say "thank you" for everything.' We even said "thank you" when they gave us a hiding.

They soon learnt I could work. I was reliable. They could give me a job and I'd do it, no matter what. I had ten hurricane lamps to clean. I cleaned the glasses, then filled the lamps with kero. I was the mailman and the milkman, too. There were lots of people who bought things from the mission. I was the only one allowed to collect mail from the Midland post-office. They sent me because I was the fastest walker.

After Albert and me had been there a while, the mission was visited by Governor Bedford. He was an Englishman. After his visit, the darker kids were separated from the lighter kids. He didn't like us being together.

They built a building close to the bridge and near the brickyard. It looked like an ark to us, so we all called it Noah's Ark. We thought that was fitting, because we was all in there together, white ones, black ones. We liked sharing that ark. Governor Bedford didn't like it one bit. He separated us all out.

The light-coloured ones had to go where the girls were, and the girls were moved to the west side of the mission.

Funny thing was, they put Freddy Lockyer in with the white kids. He had fair hair and fair skin, but really, he was a white blackfella. He wanted to stay with us blackies, he belonged to us, but they made him go. I said to him, 'You're

51

not black enough to stay with us, you have to go.' I felt sorry for him.

There was always a boundary between the girls and the boys. They had to sit one way and we had to sit the other. Apart from when we played, you had to follow the boundary and stick to your side. When the girls were older, they were put into service as housegirls and maids for anyone who wanted one. Once the boys reached adolescence, they were completely separated from the girls and put in a nearby orphanage. I suppose they were worried we might chase them.

After a while, the bigger boys started running away to Moora. They were brought back, but if they ran away a second time, the mission people would try to find work for them with the farmers up there. They were all well taught by then. I was still there when nearly all the older boys from the orphanage had run away.

Bob Coulson was another man who worked on the mission. He was a good man with a hammer. I used to watch him. If he saw any cats sneakin' around the chicken house, he'd corner them and hit them on the head with a hammer. A cat only had to look at him and he was a goner.

Coulson used to be a soldier and he often showed us his bayonet. He was full of bluff. I think he was afraid the blackfellas might tackle him one day, that's why he kept on showing us his bayonet. He always wore his shirt-sleeves rolled up, ready for action.

Corunji was Coulson's dog, a nice old dog. One day, we were going into Guildford on deliveries and Corunji followed us. We had to cross the railway line, and when a train came, old Corunji started running and barking and chasing the engine. He must have slipped, because his foot went under the wheel and his leg was cut off. We were all crying, 'Corunji, Corunji. Poor old Corunji!' We ran all the way back to the mission to tell Coulson what had happened. He got on his bike and cycled back to the railway line. We all followed. Poor old Corunji was still lyin' there, just lookin' at us as if to say, 'Can't you help me?' Coulson got off his bike, walked over to Corunji, put his hand over his snout, pulled out his hammer and hit him over the head. Then he got on his bike and cycled back to the mission. He just left him lyin' there. He did that to his own dog. Like I said, he was a good man with a hammer. I couldn't help thinking if he'd do that to his own dog, he might do that to me, one day. I didn't trust him after that.

When I was in my fourth year at the mission, Coulson caught me and some other boys outside the mission boundaries. We were playing in a picnic area near the river. It was a popular spot and we were hoping to find some money people might have dropped. When he found us, he was real mad. He ordered us back to our dormitory, he said he was going to give us a beating. You can imagine how scared we all were. He was so angry, we were frightened of what he might do to us.

We didn't go back to the dormitory, we ran all the way to Midland, to the police station. You see, the police were called Protectors of Aborigines in those days, so we thought we might get some protection from them. We all ran inside the station and told the policeman what Coulson was going to do to us. We thought he might help us, we were only kids. He listened to what we had to say, then he said, 'Get back to the mission! It's none of my business what happens to you!'

As we left the station, Coulson came riding down the road on his bike. He spotted us, rounded us up and walked us back to the mission.

By this time, he was just about boiling over. He shoved us all in a dormitory, locked the door and told us to strip off. Then, when we were naked, he raced around the dormitory like a madman, beating us with a long cane over the head and body. He didn't care where he hit us, he just beat us and beat us till we bled. There was blood everywhere. We were all crying, some of the boys were screaming: 'No more, no more. No more, master!' He liked you to call him master.

I was the only one that didn't cry out. He came over and grabbed me and said, 'Arthur, I've never had to beat you before, but *by God* I'm going to give it to you now!' He beat me and beat me, but I wouldn't cry for him. He beat me harder and harder, my thighs were running with blood and I still wouldn't cry for him. He was very, very angry, but I wasn't going to give him the satisfaction of making me cry.

After that, I decided that when my wounds were better and I could walk again, I would run away. Albert could stay there if he wanted, but I didn't want to be skinned and belted around. I'm real old now and I can still show you the scars from that beating. My wounds took a long time to heal. I was in a bad way.

I think Coulson felt guilty for beating me so hard, because, later, he took me for a train ride to visit his sister and her husband. They had a butcher's shop. It made no difference to me, I still didn't trust him. I was glad I hadn't cried for him. I was pleased that when I ran away, I'd be rid of him.

Pinjarra Frank and Tommy decided to come with me. I wanted Albert to come, but he was too frightened. He thought that if we ran away and we got caught, Coulson might beat him the way he'd beaten me.

We told all the mission kids we intended to head towards Geraldton. Other boys had run away in that direction, so it would make our story seem likely. We didn't tell anyone we really planned to head towards the goldfields. It was a good plan, because that way, if any of our friends were asked questions, they didn't have to lie.

We did run away. I must have been about fifteen or sixteen then.

Coulson didn't stay at the mission long after that. He was sacked. I guess the Anglican mob that ran the mission began to realise that all the boys were running away because of the way Coulson had been treating them. Maybe the other kids told them what Coulson had done to me.

I was sorry to leave Albert behind. After I left, he had no one to protect him and he got sick again. They sent him to hospital. Then Howden came down and took him back to Corunna Downs. As far as I know, Albert worked there until the station was sold. Then he went to Dr

Gillespie's station, Hillside.

I heard people was looking for me, I heard Howden was looking for me, but I was gone. I didn't want to be found. And I wasn't having anything more to do with school.

A Start In Life

A lot of things happened to me after I left the mission. First off, we had to cross over the railway line. We walked and walked until we came to this big tunnel. We were amazed, we'd never seen it before. We all peered down: the inside got darker and darker and there was a tiny little opening at the end. Pretty soon, a train came past. It went straight into that tunnel. We all called out, 'STOP! STOP!' but it went straight in and came out the other end with no trouble at all. We all thought a long time about that.

We walked for a long time after we crossed the railway line. We were very careful not to be seen. Finally, we got to Parkerville and camped in the bush there for a rest. Suddenly, a man appeared out of nowhere. 'What are you boys doing here?' he growled. We jumped up, scared out of our wits. We told him our story and showed him the scars on our legs. He felt sorry for us. 'Stay where you are, boys,' he said. 'I'll get you something to help you on your way.' He came back with some bread and dripping and a box of matches so we could light a fire at night and keep warm.

After that, we kept walking until it was dark. Luckily, we came across an old abandoned house. We got some dry gum leaves and sticks from the bush and lit a fire. Then we settled down for the night. There was an occupied house farther down the hill, but we'd been careful to avoid it.

We was just all driftin' off to sleep, it was a cool, clear night, when suddenly we heard a woman's voice drift by on the wind: 'I tell you, Bill, there's someone in that old house, I can see smoke coming through the roof!' We all looked up: there was no roof. We quickly put the fire out and sat close together, ready to run if we had to. Then the man's voice drifted by. 'Shut up, woman! You mind everyone's business but your own!' Their light went out and we never heard anyone. We didn't light the fire again, even though we were cold.

Early next morning, we made our way to the railway line. There was a goods train waiting there. I took my two boomerangs and walked up to the engineer. 'Please mister,' I said, 'will you swap two boomerangs for a ride on your train?' 'No!' he said.

When the train pulled out, we jumped on a wagon that was only half-full. The train passed through Northam and we finally ended up at Kellerberrin. We didn't know where the train was headed, but riding on that wagon was a lot better than walking.

At Kellerberrin station, the station master spotted us. He came running over and hauled us down. 'You're the boys that are wanted by the police, aren't you?' he said. He had his hand on my shoulder. I wondered what he was going to do with us. He looked us over real good and then said, 'Right boys, you see that building over there, that's the police station. I want you boys to go and present yourselves to the constable, he'll know what to do with you.'

He pointed again to the small building farther down the track and sent us on our way. We walked slowly down the track, we wasn't sure if he was watching us or not. When we got near some bush, we veered off and ran for our lives.

No one chased after us. We were starving hungry by then. We found some mouldy bread and an old milk can. We ate the bread and scraped out what was left from inside of the can, then we set off again.

We kept following the railway line. Just as the sun was setting, we reached Hines Hill. We were dog-tired by then. We sat down at the bottom of a hill to rest. Suddenly, we spotted a tall man coming slowly down the hill towards us. The sun was in our eyes, so we were frightened he was a policeman, but we were too tired to get up and run.

He walked right up and said, 'What are you boys doing here? Where have you come from?' We told him our story, he looked at the scars on our legs and shook his head. He told us he was a farmer. We asked him if he could give us some flour to make damper, and some tea and sugar. He went away and came back with some tucker. He warned us to be careful, he said the police had been asking about us.

After he left, we built a fire in the bush. We wanted to fill our bellies real quick. Just as we were making damper, another man appeared from nowhere and shouted, 'What are you boys up to?' He said he was the station master from Hines Hill and he'd spotted our smoke and tracked us down. We were scared, tired and starving, we didn't have the heart or the strength to run away. We waited for him to tell us he was going to turn us in to the police. He walked up close to us and looked us up and down. 'Where'd you boys get those scars?' We told him our story and he took pity on us.

'Put out that fire, boys,' he said. 'I'll take you to a friend of mine. You'll eat better there.'

We followed him through the bush; we were too tired to care where he took us. We ended up at a small house. It was owned by a contractor, a man who worked around the nearby properties. He was a widower with three daughters. They sat us down at a table inside the house. They took us inside, just like that. Wasn't that something? The girls giggled when they looked at us. They cooked us a big meal and we were allowed to eat as much as we liked. Can you believe that? They even let us sleep the night there.

The next morning, Tommy decided to strike off by himself. He was from the goldfields and he wanted to get back home. He missed his people. Pinjarra Frank and me didn't know what to do. We thought we'd just keep on walking.

Then the contractor came to us and said, 'Boys, how'd you like to stay with me for two weeks and help with some fencing? I can't pay you, but you'll have your tucker.' That was good enough for us. We didn't have anywhere else to go.

We helped with the fencing and whatever else he wanted doing. The two weeks turned into a month and we were still there. The girls cooked us good meals. They were allowed to play with me, but not with Pinjarra Frank. He was real dark and he didn't work as hard as me.

One day, a man came by. He was a good-looking man with a big moustache. He came in a sulky, all dressed up. At first, when I saw him coming, I thought he was a policeman, and I nearly ran away. He pulled up at the house and said to the contractor, 'I'm after a boy who can ride. I hear you've got two boys, can they ride? There's jobs going if they can.'

'I can ride,' I said. I prayed the horse wouldn't throw me as soon as I jumped on. The contractor said, 'Stay with us, we're fond of you. Let Pinjarra go.' He was a good man, that contractor, but his house was close to the railway line and, all the time I'd been there, I'd been lookin' over my shoulder, wonderin' when the police would catch up with me. I decided to go with the stranger. McQuarie was his name.

McQuarie climbed down from the sulky and unhitched two horses from the back. 'On you get,' he said. Pinjarra leapt on, but they had to give me a leg up, I was too small. I clung on to the reins and mane and prayed with all my heart I wouldn't fall off. For twenty-five miles, McQuarie drove the sulky, and for twenty-five miles, I bumped up and down, barely hanging in the saddle. Jig-jog, I went. My bottom and the insides of my legs were painful sore. I kept telling myself the next hill would be the last one, but they kept going on and on. We went through forest country, then one more hill, then Nungarin. The sun had set by then. That was my first start in life.

The next day, McQuarie's son Ernie came to me and said, 'Come on, I'll show you the ropes. I hear you need some riding lessons.' That day, I learnt to canter so my body didn't jolt around so much. My legs and bottom were still sore, but I wasn't giving up that easy.

Ernie took me out to one of the runs and we stopped at a lake. He reined his horse in, climbed down and lay on the grass. I did the same. I thought he was going to tell me about the run. He said nothing. He pulled his hat down over his eyes, took out a plug of tobacco from his pouch and rolled a big, fat cigarette. Then he smoked it real slow. All the time, he was looking at the lake. When he finished, I sat up. I thought, now he's going to tell me about the run. He didn't even look at me, he just lay back, pulled a book out from his pocket, and started to read. He turned each page real slow and deliberate like. I sat looking at the lake. We stayed like that all day, not talking, just lying there. When it was dark, he said, 'Right, let's go.' They were the only words he said to me. We rode back to the station and had tucker.

I had tucker in the kitchen. The white workers sat at one table, the blacks at another. McQuarie and his family ate in the formal dining-room. That night, I slept in the stripper. I lifted up the top and crawled inside. Later, I got an old sheepskin for a mattress and sometimes I had a blanket, too, if there was one to spare. Later on, they floored the barn ready for barn dances and I slept in there with the horses. I reckon I must have slept in that barn for well over two years.

The following day, Ernie took me to a different run. It was a long way out. By and by, he reined in his horse, climbed down and sat on the ground. He pulled out a plug of tobacco and rolled another big, fat cigarette. We did the same thing we had the day before.

The third day was the same, except in a different place. I soon learnt that Ernie was not only lazy, but greedy, too. He never shared anything. Not his tobacco, not his food, nothing. You could be starving and he wouldn't offer you anything. Later on, McQuarie built a store and Ernie would sneak in there and eat big tins of peaches when we were supposed to be boundary riding. He never offered me a drop. He'd open up a big tin of peaches and scoop them out with a spoon. He'd lean against the counter, look me straight in the eye and eat some more.

Eventually, Ernie ran the store and all the farmers who lived nearby bought on credit, payable after harvest. No one paid their debts, Ernie kept on eating and eating and the store went bankrupt.

As for me, I decided never to worry about tucker. When I was out all day, minding the cattle, they only gave me one piece of bread and a thin slice of pork. The meat was so thin that if you held it up to the sun, you could see through it.

After I'd been there a while, McQuarie told me I was now a stockman. From then on, I took my orders from him. He said my conditions were five bob a year, my horse and saddle, board and tucker. I never did get that five bob a year, but I wasn't worried about wages. I had a home.

In three years, I was head stockman and mustering cattle all over the district. It was pioneer days then. They were just clearing Nungarin and the railway line wasn't even there.

When there was no stock work to be done, I spent my time grubbing boab tea-tree and clearing more land ready for cropping. Other times, I did errands for McQuarie, driving him and his friends here and there in the sulky.

All this time, I went under the name of 'Marble'. I thought it might give me some protection from the police, they were still looking for me. McQuarie told me, 'Marble, if you ever see the police round here, you hide, and I'll tell them to take Pinjarra Frank instead.'

McQuarie reckoned Pinjarra didn't work as hard as me. Thing was, they didn't want him, he was real black. They wanted me.

Even though Pinjarra was older than me, I was his boss. Pinjarra was lazy, and in the end, McQuarie gave him the sack.

McQuarie was a good man, he never growled at me. I remember once, I was in the barn putting blinkers on a horse, I had to climb up onto the manger to do it. I was only small. It took me a long time to grow. McQuarie came in and saw me and laughed, 'Hey, Marble,' he said, 'when are you going to grow?' I didn't say nothin'. I was like a tree that never been watered. I just thought to myself, yeah, I don't get enough to eat. Dick McQuarie, the other son, used to give me clothes. They were always too big, but I just rolled them up till I grew into them. They fitted me for years.

Sometimes, McQuarie would ask me to drive a visitor around or help someone with work they were doing. Everyone wanted me in those days.

I remember this fella Baird. He owned a shop in Perth.

They call it Myers, these days. It used to be called Bairds. He came to Nungarin once to help build a house for his brother. I took him out with his tools and he got interested in me. One day, he said, 'Would you like to come to Perth, Marble? I'll look after you, give you a good schooling.' I started to think about that hiding I got at the mission. That was supposed to be schooling. I thought, nobody's going to school me again. Now, if he had've said, 'Marble, what if I take you back to Corunna Downs?' I might have gone, but school, that was where they gave you a good hiding for doing nothing. Seems funny, thinking about it all now. If I'd have taken his offer, I might have ended up as a shopwalker for Bairds.

I decided to stay with McQuarie. He never said, 'How long are you gunna be?' I was my own boss. He never gave me any money but I didn't worry about it. I was just growing up and there was nothing to spend money on.

One chap McQuarie had me drive around was Syd Stock, a big squatter from Victoria. I had to take him by buggy to his brothers in Nungarin. One night, we was sitting by the fire when he turned to me and said, 'Would you like to come back to Victoria with me, Marble? I've got stations there and horses and buggies, too. You can work on one of my stations.' I looked at him, he was a good man. The kind of man I liked. Then I said, 'No. I don't want to go far away from the north. I might never come back. This land is my home.'

Now, that could have been an opportunity missed. He was an old man and he trusted me. He might have given me a station. I knew he was a good man, because whenever we went to the hotel, he never put me outside like most white men. Where he went, I went. He kept me with him always. Treated me like his equal. That was a rare thing in those days. A thing to be treasured.

Everybody seemed to like me, then. I couldn't make out why. I'd look in a mirror and what'd I see? Me. An ugly bloke like me. What did they see in me?

One day, Dick said to me, 'Come on, Marble, we'll take you to the Northam Show.' They gave me new clothes and everything. They stayed in their Aunty's pub, the Shamrock Hotel, and I camped in the horses' manger nearby.

I loved that Show. They had merry-go-rounds and all sorts of things I hadn't seen before. That was the only time I hit the boss for some money. Dick said to the boss, 'Give me some money,' so I said, 'Me too, boss.' He gave me half a sovereign. When we got to the races, I gave it to a bloke to put on a winner for me. I never saw that half-sovereign again.

I had to watch from outside, they said I didn't have enough money to bet and pay my entry fee to the races as well. Inside, they had two big pots of hot dogs boiling up. I could smell them and I was real hungry. My money was gone, so what could I do.

1911 was a good harvest for nearly everyone. It was never as good after that. Dry conditions seemed to set in. Good rain fell in some places, like Bruce Rock. The farmers there were getting two bags to the acre, but it was lighter soil. If you were cropping in heavy soil, it was like trying to plough without hitching up the horses. Things got bad and we took three hundred head of cattle farther north, trying to find better grazing and water.

In July 1912, miners were finding gold at Paynes Find. There was traffic on the roads. When the bit of water we found finally dried up, we took the cattle back to Nungarin. In the end, we had to sell most of them.

We kept working McQuarie's station, but things got worse and worse. The first time McQuarie went broke was because everyone owed him money. All the farmers were in debt to him and none of them could pay their bills. The bailiff came to sell off the stock and the machinery. All the other farmers got together and agreed not to bid against McQuarie. He used his sister's money and got everything back for ten shillings or a pound. The bailiff didn't know what to do. McQuarie was the only one bidding, the others were just standing around, watching.

After that first time, McQuarie got the other farmers to

help him clear a lot of land for extra cropping. He was going to get just enough out of that crop to pay his bills. Jackatee and me cleared even more land and put in more crops. We pulled out big boab trees, raked the roots together and burnt them. Then we put the crop in. Jackatee was a good worker. He was real black. At night, we'd boil our billy in the bush and cook pancakes for tea on the forge. That was all the tucker we had. He was a good friend, old Jackatee.

Anyway, turned out the crop was better than before, but still not good enough to save McQuarie. A bad drought came and finished him off. There was no water, no feed for the animals. Dick and me had to shoot poor old Bess. She was a good horse, but there was nothin' for her to eat. What stock was left was in bad condition. Some of them were too far gone to be helped.

McQuarie said to Dick, 'Dick, you can stop on the station. There's plenty of seed and super. You could put in another crop.' Dick said, 'No fear, I'm not doin' that. There's a war comin', I'm off to fight.' Ernie left, too.

I stopped with McQuarie till he was real broke. The farmers still owed him money and the bailiff was coming again. Dalgetys sold him up. They didn't worry about the man battling on the land, they just wanted their money. If the land didn't come into fruition like it should, they sold you up. I finally left with Jackatee in 1913.

We went into Nungarin, trying to find work. We'd do anything. One chap saw us in the street and asked us to help him load a truck. He gave us threepence. Threepence, for all that work! We bought some bread and ate it. We were starvin' hungry. A big load of sandalwood came in and the storekeeper came over and said, 'You boys want work loading that sandalwood?'

'Yes,' we said. We were desperate, we didn't ask the pay.

When we finished loading twelve ton of sandalwood, he gave us half a crown. Then we gave it back to him in his store for some sardines and biscuits and that was the end of that. It seems like the whitefella doesn't want the blackfella to get a foot in this world.

I had no money, no job. I was about twenty, twenty-one then. I could see I couldn't live in Nungarin. I decided to strike out for Goomalling. There were two friends of mine who wanted to go there, too, Billy One Moon and Hunting Maggie. Hunting Maggie was blind. Billy was her husband and he used to lead her along the road with a stick. I called them Aunty and Uncle. I wasn't in my home country and I thought if any other natives asked who I was, it would give me some protection.

By the time we were three or four miles out of Nungarin, McQuarie pulled up behind us in a buggy. 'Hey, Marble,' he said, 'I want you to drive me to Hines Hill and the bailiff wants a boy to help round up stock.'

'Righto,' I said. I told my friends I would meet them later.

After I got back from Hines Hill, I rounded up the stock. They were no trouble. I had a bad time with my old pony. She wanted to stop with me. She didn't want to go in the corral with the others. I thought McQuarie might say, 'Take her, Marble, she's your horse,' but he didn't. I nearly cried when I saw her go.

After that, the bailiff said, 'You want another job?'

'Too right,' I said.

'Good. I want you to shepherd the sheep near the pub till we're ready to truck 'em.'

While I was minding the sheep, a man came up and spoke to me.

'When you finished working for that bailiff, how about coming and working for me? I'll give you ten bob a week plus board.'

'That's all right by me!' I said. It was the most I ever been offered.

After they trucked the sheep, the bailiff gave me thirty shillings. That was more than I expected. I picked up my swag and went over and saw Dick McQuarie.

'Dick,' I said, 'how much you want for that old bike of yours?'

'My old bike? Well, let me see, about thirty bob would do.'

I gave him my thirty bob and wheeled the bike across the

railway line to Hancock's place. A local had imported the bike years ago from England and sold it to Dick. It had no tyres or tubes. I didn't mind. I had a bike and I was looking forward to my new job.

Not Afraid To Work

From 1913 till 1916, I worked for Hancock. In all that time, I got no pay, only my tucker, and I worked damn hard. I never saw that ten bob a week he promised me. Most of the time I was there, I was freezing cold. We lived in an old bough shed. There was no proper place to sleep, and in winter the wind cut right through you. I used to get old gallon tins, fill them with hot water, tie bags around them, then strap them to my feet. My feet felt the cold the most. Like ice, they were. I never had shoes. I tell you, it's hard to keep warm in an open bough shed.

Most of my working time was spent clearing the land, seeding and cropping. It was hard work, but I was used to it. In between times, I made mud bricks for a hut with a chimney and fireplace. I used to tread the mud with my bare feet, and when a stick tickled my foot, I'd pull it out. If I didn't, the brick would crack. The bricks started to mount up. We dug out a hole in the ground and I built a cellar with a nice big chimney inside to throw out the heat. Winter came and we'd used all the bricks, so we slept in the cellar. It sure was warmer than that shed. I felt like a king that winter.

While I was at Hancock's, I managed to get tyres and tubes for my bike. I fixed that bike up real good, oiled it and kept it nice. In my spare time I'd ride all over the countryside, wherever my legs would take me, round and round they'd go, pushing those pedals to goodness knows where. I never planned on going anywhere in particular. I just liked riding round, looking at the land and the bush. It was what you'd call my entertainment. I met lots of different people when I was out.

'Gidday,' they'd say, or, 'Mornin'.' Course, you got some that weren't interested in talkin' to you, but I never let them worry me. I loved that bike, it made me feel real grand.

It was during my time at Hancock's that I met up with a Welshman named Davy Jones. He was working on the Trans Line, out on the Nullarbor Plain, and now and then he came to Nungarin to check on his land. It was at the time when Lord Kitchener had ordered all the States to be linked by railway line, in case of war. That way, they could help each other.

While Davy was working the Trans Line, the Land Department was trying to forfeit his land in Nungarin. That's why he visited Hancock so much. Davy couldn't write, so he'd get Hancock to send letters for him. Excuses and reasons about why he was away and how he'd be working the land once the Trans Line was finished.

He didn't just talk to Hancock, he talked to me as well. He seemed real friendly. More like a white blackfella, really. Sometimes when the three of us were together, I'd show off. I wasn't big, but I was strong and good with an axe. I'd say to Hancock and Davy, 'I'll drop this big tree with my axe before you even get back to camp.' Camp was about twenty feet away. They'd laugh and walk off, but I always did it. I wasn't afraid of work.

Towards the end of three years with Hancock, I could see I wasn't getting anywhere. The hut was built by then, but I was still just getting me tucker, no money. I wasn't going nowhere.

'Hancock,' I said to him one day, 'how about paying me that money you owe me?' He went real quiet and looked at me. The year was 1916, it was the middle of winter and there was a flood. After a while, he said, 'Marble, you clear that forty acres of land I been wantin' cleared and I'll give you twelve pounds, no more, no less!'

Now he'd tried to get all sorts of people to clear that land. Nobody could do it. It was covered with big logs and stumps, and with the flood on, it was worth more like one hundred pounds, not twelve pounds! Trouble was, I knew he had me and he knew, too. Where could I go? I had no money, no home. 'Right,' I said, 'I'll clear the land for you, as long as you pay me. For three years I been working for you, breaking my back and you never paid me yet. I got no choice, I got to stick with you or I got nothing.'

I don't think he believed I'd clear the land. He thought he'd have me there three more years, doing his work for him, building his house. He didn't know me. I worked from three hours before sunrise till sunset, clearing and burning. During that time, the flood got worse and the railway line was nearly washed away. Every day I was soaking wet. My feet were like blocks of ice. Sometimes the rain drove down so hard I couldn't see in front of me, but I kept going. I wasn't going to give up, it was my only way out. The job took me three weeks. I cleared that land by myself when no other man would, or could.

I showed Hancock the land, then asked him for my money. He couldn't believe I'd done it. He didn't give me the money right away, he kept me waiting, waiting, hoping I'd forget about it. He knew I'd leave soon as he gave me the money. I kept asking him for my pay. In the end, he went to Perth and got the money from the bank. He took out fifteen shillings a week board for the three weeks it had taken me to clear the land.

Despite the flood, 1916 was a good year for most farmers. When Micky Farrell heard I'd left Hancock, he offered me work carting two hundred tons of chaff for twenty-five shillings a week. There were two wagons and a steam cutter and fifteen men on the job, but only me doing the carting. The work with Micky only lasted two weeks. After that, I was looking for work again. Mr Williams gave me a job harvesting. I got two pounds a week for that. When that job wound up, I didn't know what I was going to do. I just hoped something would turn up. That was when I met up with Davy Jones again. I hadn't seen him for quite a while. He told me he'd finished working on the Trans Line.

'Marble,' he said, 'why don't you come share-farming with me? You buy the horses and harness and come and work my land with me.'

'All right, Dave,' I said, 'that suits me fine.' I had nothing else to do. I bought the horses and the harness and teamed up with Davy Jones.

He would've been stuck if he hadn't got me. He was a failure. He'd tried cropping his land before. When I started with Davy, I put in two hundred acres with my team. They were a good team, hard-working animals. As hard as me. I bought their feed and watered them and looked after them real well. That year, we had the best crops in the district. One paddock gave ten bags to the acre, the other seven bags. The lowest yield we got was eighteen bushels to the acre. From then on, we never looked back. All our crops were bumpers, right through till 1923.

Davy Jones became Mr Davy Jones of the Nungarin district. He was independent now. He didn't have to work for no one. When he was working on the Trans Line, he had a tiny little purse he kept with him in camp. It had all his money in it. Now, he was banking with Lloyds of London. He had money in his pockets and I had money in mine, but not as much. It was his land, but I did all the work. The only thing I owned was the team. My share after harvest was one quarter, Davy got the rest.

I saved all my money, never spent a penny. Pretty soon, I had enough to buy a farm. I bought a nice little farm in Mukinbudin.

I'll never forget Mucka when I first saw it. There was nothing there. A few houses now and then, but nothing more. Later, I had the first truck there and I used to cart water for the townspeople from ten miles out. They didn't even have a pub till years later.

My name was good right through the district. Everyone knew I was a good worker. Later, I had six men working for me, clearing my land. I paid them out of a cheque book. I was the only farmer in the area to have a cheque book. All the other farmers were mortgaged to the bank, they had no say in their crop. They were jealous of me, a black man, doing better than what they were. When I first bought the farm, they all made fun of me. 'Where are you going to get stock from?' they'd call. 'What would you know about farming?' they'd yell. They thought I knew nothin'. I proved them wrong.

Anyway, before long I was working my own farm as well as share-farming with Davy. Things were going real well for me. One day, Davy came up to me and said, 'Listen Marble, you've got your farm in Mucka now, what about if you just stick to that and I give Bill Bradley a go. You know, the bloke that's working for Hull's. I'd like to share-farm with him.'

I didn't know what to say. Davy was my friend. It wasn't that I was thinking about the extra money, it just seemed that Davy didn't want me with him any more, after so long together. Davy was standing there and I kept looking at the ground. In the end, I said, 'All right Dave, if that's the way you want it, I can pull out and go home.'

That year, I put in my last crop with Davy. Bill and Mrs Bradley moved in with Davy while the crop was still growing.

Every Sunday, Mrs Bradley would come out and look over the crop. 'Ooh, what a lovely crop, Marble,' she would say.

One day, she said to Davy, 'Mr Jones, look at them clouds up there, it looks like they could bring a hailstorm.'

'You don't know what you're talking about, woman, we don't get no hailstorms round here,' said Davy.

That was Sunday morning. Ten o'clock Sunday night, the rain came, and the thunder and lightning and the hail, as well. The hail took the crop right off. There wasn't one head left, even the trees were stripped bare. They looked dead, standing there with no leaves on.

Davy heard the noise of the hail. It was pitch-black outside apart from the lightning. He'd been sitting by the fire when it started, and when the hail came, he didn't even stop to put on a coat. Just lit up the lantern and rushed down to the crop. There he was in the pouring rain, running up and down, in and out, trying to see how many heads were left. All you could see was his lantern bobbing up and down. The lightning flashed once and I saw him. He was soaking wet. He couldn't believe it was really hailing.

I think God must have been looking after me. Something told me to get insured that year. I had never been insured before. I came out with my quarter and Dave got nothing.

Davy's bad luck continued. The next year, he put his own crop in, but forgot to seed with super, and it died off. The following year, Bill Bradley put the crop in for him, but Davy was in the same position he was in before he joined up with me. He still had no team, so this meant he had to take off Hull's crop and Micky Farrell's before he could have the use of their team to take off his own crop. He only just made it in time.

If Davy had've stuck with me, I'd have had his crop off early on and my own as well. No one could work a team the way I could. It was me that gave him his start. I did all the work, he just stood back and collected the money.

By the time the thirties came round and the Depression hit, he wanted me back. I was married by then. I had responsibilities. Davy said, 'You can bring your wife, too, Arthur.'

I was going by my real name, now. I left 'Marble' behind when I left Davy. Now I was Arthur Corunna, farmer, of Mukinbudin.

My Little Sister

After I left Davy in the twenties, some important things happened to me. In 1925, I went down to Perth. I'd heard that my little sister Daisy was living at Ivanhoe. Ivanhoe was a big house in Claremont on the banks of the Swan River. Daisy was a servant there, living with our father, Howden Drake-Brockman, and his second wife, Alice.

I was keen to see Daisy again. She was my sister, my family. I wanted my little sister Daisy to know she had a brother who was getting on in the world.

I hardly recognised her when I saw her. When they took me from Corunna Downs, she was only a baby, with real white blonde hair. Now, here she was, a grown woman, with black frizzy hair. She was small and pretty, like our mother, Annie. I was sure glad to see her.

When I first called in at Ivanhoe, Mrs Drake-Brockman was out. Later that day, she came home to find me sitting in the kitchen doorway, talking to Daisy, my legs stretched out onto the verandah. You see, I'd finally started to grow. I was a big man. I wasn't small no more.

I took to visiting Daisy as often as I could. One year, I hired a buggy and pair for two shillings and took her to the Show. We thought we were real grand. I took her to the races, on picnics, everywhere. Daisy loved the horses. Nothing she liked better than seeing those wonderful animals go for their lives round the track. We both loved horses. Helen Bunda, our cousin, used to come as well. She was in service with another white family. She did the most beautiful needlework. She was a clever woman with her hands.

Judith, June and Dick Drake-Brockman were only little then. I used to give them horsey rides when I was at Ivanhoe and scare them by chasing them round the lawn. Daisy was their nursemaid.

On one of my visits to Ivanhoe, Alice Drake-Brockman gave me a little dog. She didn't want it. I called him Pixie. I took that little dog with me wherever I went. He was a good little dog. I've always had a tender spot for little creatures like that.

When I saw Daisy again in 1925, it was also the first time I'd seen Howden since I'd run away. I wondered what he'd say to me. I wondered if I'd be welcome. Mrs Drake-Brockman said I could sleep with Daisy in her room. When Howden came home, he came straight to Daisy's room. He knocked on the door, came in and shook me by the hand real hard. He hadn't changed. He looked older, more tired, but apart from that, he was just the same. I was a grown man now. We were both men. 'I'm pleased to see you, Arthur,' he said. I didn't know what to say.

After that, whenever I stayed in Perth, I always slept in Daisy's room. At night, we had long talks, catching up on the news. I went and saw a lawyer and made a will, leaving all my earthly goods to Daisy. I wasn't married then. She was my only family.

Sometimes when I was in Perth, I'd ride on the electric trams. *DING! DING! DING!* they'd call out, then change back the other way. I wasn't going nowhere in particular, I just loved to listen to that noise. I went on the trains, too. In those days, you could go from Merredin to Perth for seventeen shillings. From Kununoppin to Perth was the same. I loved riding on the trains. I felt like I was someone important, being able to get on, pay my fare and sit there like a king until I got off at the next stop.

In 1927, I got a letter from Howden. I hadn't seen Daisy for a while. I'd been busy on the farm. The letter asked if I'd like to have Daisy with me. It said they didn't want her no more and they wondered if I could come and get her. Too right, I thought. Nothing I'd like better.

I went over and talked to one of my neighbours. He was a white man, but a good man, young and single. He was well off, too, and I knew he'd treat Daisy right. I asked him if he wanted a wife. He asked who I had in mind. I told him about Daisy and how pretty she was, how hard she worked and what a good wife she'd make. He said, 'Arthur, any sister of yours is all right by me.' I knew I had him then. I didn't want Daisy just marrying anyone. I wanted someone I could trust, someone who would treat her real nice. She was my family. My little sister.

I finished what I had to do on the farm and was all set to get Daisy when another letter arrived. It said they'd changed their minds and I couldn't have her after all. I was disappointed. So was the farmer next door.

In December that year, I heard Daisy had had a baby girl. It was news to me. I wondered, then, if that was why they'd changed their minds. I'd have had her still. I wish she'd come to me, baby and all. I love kids.

72

Early in 1928, Howden died. He'd been a sick man for some time. Personally, I think he left his heart in Corunna. Howden saw Daisy's baby before he died. They called her Gladys. He held her in his arms and said, 'She's very beautiful.' She was one of the most beautiful babies I'd ever seen.

Shortly before his death, Howden mailed me a whole pile of photos that had been taken on Corunna Downs. I guess Howden figured no one else would want old pictures. It was the only thing he ever gave me.

The other thing I discovered in the twenties was boxing. Boxing and wrestling. I was good at both, but I didn't know it till then. When I was a kid, old Fred Stream learned me a bit. He knew they were going to send me to the mission and he reckoned if I didn't learn something, I'd get a hiding.

I was a farmer, I wasn't trained for fighting, but one punch from me and I could flatten them. I used to know Riley. His son was a referee and he had a boxing and wrestling tent. He used to travel all round Perth and up the Nor'west.

Riley said, 'If I trained you, I reckon you'd be middle-weight champion of the world.' They always let me in the Show free because they knew I was a good fighter.

Whenever the Shows came round Nungarin, I'd put in for the boxing and wrestling. Sometimes they were too scared to take me on. I remember one bloke took a long look at me and then said, 'I'm not taking you on, mate. I seen a bloke look like you once before. He gave me a terrible time.'

One year in the late twenties, the hotel manager from Mucka said, 'Arthur, you want to take my beer on your truck into the Show and sell it for me?' I was one of the few men who had a truck in the district. I thought, why not? I loaded up the truck, threw a tarp over the grog and drove to Nungarin. I spent the night in the hotel there. Everything was booked up to the pub in Mucka, my board and tucker. I was a white man, then, not black. It was a king's life.

Once inside the Show, I sold the beer from the truck, and

all the time, I could hear these men, singing out, singing out. They were boxers and wrestlers and they were singing out for men to come and challenge them. When all the beer was sold, I thought, I'll have a go. I walked over, put my hand up and yelled, 'Hey! Over here, I'll have a go!'

While I was standing there, a bloke came up to me and pushed me on the shoulder. He was one of the trainers. I'd seen him before.

'You can't wrestle, mate,' he said. I just grabbed him, clothes and all. Lifted him up and dropped him. Pinned him to the dirt.

'What do you think of yourself now, mate?' I said. He went for his life, dirt all over him. The men in the ring had seen what happened and they wouldn't take me on after that. I looked too tough.

There was a boxer I remember well, Jack Yakem. He was white and he fought in the Royal Show, everywhere. He lived for fighting. He used to stick out his chest and strut round the ring like a rooster round the hens and yell out, 'My name's Jack Yakem! I *CRACK* 'em, you *STACK* 'em.' Everyone was scared of him. Anyway, he was the same weight as me and I thought, Arthur...have a go.

When they let me into the ring, the crowd was full round us, urging us on, calling out. They all wanted to see me get beat. Jack didn't waste no time. He started pummelling me in the ribs with his fists.

After a few minutes I thought, I've had enough of this. I hit him fair over the earhole and dropped him right there. He went flying, flat to the ground. The crowd roared. Anyhow, he got up and I dropped him again. Eleven times I dropped him, quick with my fists. I won that fight, but they never gave me any money. It was always the same. When I got home, I took my singlet off, I was black and blue all round my ribs where he'd pummelled me. I don't know what colour he was.

I was a hard nut to crack, when I was young. My life was full of sport.

Mukinbudin

When I was young, I had girls runnin' after me all the time. I was a good catch and they all wanted me. Trouble is, I was like my old grandfather, tender-hearted. I wouldn't go with any girl, because if I got her into trouble, I'd have to marry her. Other blokes were different. They'd take a girl out, get her into trouble, then let her go.

In the old days, when they announced your engagement, they took your photo and everything and put it in the paper. I was worried about that. I thought to myself, when I get engaged, what can I say? Who could I say I was and who was my father? I decided I'd trick them all. If they ask me, I'd say, 'My father is Mr Corunna from Corunna Downs Station.' That's what I would put in the paper and no one would know any better. No one would know about Howden and Annie and how they wasn't married white man's way. You see, they were very particular about such things in those days.

There were times when I could have protected myself through the name of Brockman, but I never did. Howden never gave me nothin'. I've only got one good Father and He's in heaven. No matter which way the wind's blowin', He's there with you.

Before I married my wife, Adeline, she came to me and said, 'Arthur, I've seen a fortune-teller and she told me I'm going to marry you. She also told me what your life will be like and that one day somebody will rob you of your farm.'

I said, 'Nobody's goin' to rob me. They'll get this fist if they try!' I was gettin' on in years, about thirty-five, and I'd been thinkin' I should marry, but when Adeline said that, I thought, better not get married or I'll be losin' my farm.

Still, I couldn't stay single for ever, so I thought the only fair way was to put all the girls' names in a hat. I figured the name that I picked out would be my wife. Me and my mates put all the girls' names we knew into an old felt hat. I thought Helen Bunda's name could come out. She was my cousin and her name was in there. I wanted a small girl, not a big woman. Someone like my mother.

One of my mates held the hat up and I picked out a slip. On it was written *Adeline Wilks*!

'That can't be the one,' I said, 'she's plump. Let me have another go.'

We mixed the papers round real good, they held up the hat and I chose another one. *Adeline Wilks* again.

'Those papers ain't mixed up right,' I said, 'give me one more go.' This time, we gave those papers a mixin' they'll never forget. They held up the hat once more.

'Last time,' I said. I closed my eyes, put my hand in and pulled out a slip. *Adeline Wilks*! I gave up.

'Well, if she's the one I got to have, so be it,' I said. I think the spirit of her people must have chosen her for me.

We were married in the early thirties in Perth, in St Marys Cathedral, by Bishop Prindiville. She was a Catholic and I was an Anglican. I agreed to bring up the little ones as Catholics. It didn't seem important — all one God, after all.

Shortly after we were married, I was out in the paddock, diggin' roots. It was a hot day, the sweat was pourin' off me. Anyhow, I was diggin' away, diggin' away, when, suddenly, I was struck blind. I closed my eyes and opened them, but I couldn't see nothin'. I closed my eyes real tight and opened them again, but I still couldn't see. I could feel my hand on my face, but I couldn't see it. I sat down and closed my eyes and stayed there for a while, real still like.

That's when I knew Annie was dead. My poor old mother who I hadn't seen since they took me away was dead. I stood up and opened my eyes, I could see again, but Annie was dead. She was so small and pretty, I wish I'd seen her again, just one more time.

The first farm I had in Mukinbudin was hard work. My house was only a bit of tin. No electricity or water. We had to go over the line if we wanted water.

I was on my own, a black man with no one to help him. I done all the fencing myself, the dam, too. Paid money to men to clear land. I made sure I owed no one, I didn't want no mortgage. You mortgage a place and you're beat. They've got you then, just over a lousy little bit of money.

After I'd improved the farm, a bloke wanted to buy it. Jack Edwards was his name. He already had other farms and he wanted mine as well. You see, the white man gets greedy, he wants to take everything.

We sold the farm bare for four thousand pounds. He told me he wanted to rent it for so many years till he got his money together. So he gave me four hundred pounds the first year and said he couldn't give me any more till he'd made some more money out of my farm so he could pay for it. There was no stipulation in our agreement that my horses and machinery went with the land, but soon I found he was takin' my horses and machinery and workin' his other farms with them as well as mine. He put in one season and had a good crop, but the following year, the Depression hit and he said he couldn't go through with the sale.

I said, 'Well, Jack, if you can't go through with it, you replace everything on the farm the same as you got it, the horses in the same quantity, the machinery in good gear, collars and harness and everything.' Two horses he never replaced, I let him off on that.

With the Depression, the price of wheat fell to ten shillings a bushel and then to five shillings. I had two boys, Arthur and Manfred, by then, and in 1934, my third son, Albert, was born. My crop yielded eight bags to the acre that year, but at five bob a bushel it didn't amount to much. All we got out of it was a pram for Albert.

In 1936, my daughter Norma was born. Life was real hard. I'd do anything to make a few bob; anything to keep my wife and family. I picked roots at a shilling an acre, I cleared five hundred acres of mallees* for seven pounds. I burnt

* *mallee* — various Australian species of *Eucalyptus,* having a number of almost unbranched stems arising from a large underground root stock. Found mainly in semi-arid regions. Also an area of scrub land where the predominant species of plant is mallee.

mallees for charcoal to sell to gas producers. By gee, some men were mean, then, they'd pinch my roots and my charcoal. I was doin' the work and they was gettin' the profits.

Ever since the Depression, I've voted Labor. When the Labor Government got into power, we got another two shillings a bushel.

It was during this time that I owed money on my header*. I was the first farmer in the district to have a truck and the first to buy a header. My header came down by train. Tug Wilson, who ran the post-office at Mucka and was also an agent for Wesfarmers, took a photo of it. I was makin' history.

I think I must have been somethin' out of the ordinary, to be a black man ahead of everybody else.

Anyway, Wesfarmers summonsed me over the header. When Wesfarmers first started, I bought me bags, me super, everything, off them and I paid them every time. It was little men like me that made Wesfarmers.

First, a policeman came and said, 'We've got to sell you up!'

'Oh yeah,' I said, 'what are you goin' to sell?'

'All your goods and chattels.'

I laughed. 'You needn't worry about that,' I said, 'I got no goods and chattels!'

Anyway, when the summons came, I went down to Perth to see a lawyer who came from Bunbury, Howard Barth. He rang Wesfarmers and said, 'Believe you're takin' Corunna on about the debt he has. You want to fight him, you have to push it through me.'

I could have stuck to the header, if I'd wanted. I had a good crop and was goin' to use it to take it off. In the end, I said, 'Take the rubbish of a thing away!' I'd never had any debt with them before, I'd always paid my way.

* *header* — a form of reaping machine which cuts off and gathers only the head of a grain crop.

Later on, during the Depression, the Agricultural Bank served a summons on me for owin' them one thousand three hundred pounds, I'd had to mortgage my farm with them to get by. They sold up everything, all my machinery. But not my horses. I had nowhere to keep them, they were strayin' everywhere and the bloke who'd taken on my farm said he was goin' to shoot them if I didn't take care of them. I had to round them up and sell them for three pounds a head to be shot for pig feed. Can you tell me that was fair, for all my pioneering days, to be treated like that?

The Depression didn't do no favours for my neighbour who'd had four farms, either. He had to sell up, he left the district for good. I had to take my family and start again on new, uncleared land. It's hard for the black man to get ahead.

My neighbours in Mucka were a mixed bag, some good, some very bad. There was a man that give me a lot of trouble, he was mean, he didn't like blacks. That man used to shoot my horses and pigs.

One day, he was in town and he said to one of my neighbours, 'Have you managed to get Arthur off his farm yet?' He went on and on, talkin' to my neighbour about how two white men can easily get rid of one black man. My neighbour never said a word, he just let him ramble on, then he said, 'You're talkin' to the wrong bloke. I don't want Arthur off his farm.'

You see, this man was my friend. I'd helped him when things went wrong. When he was in hospital, I'd helped cut his hay and shear his sheep. He was my mate. Whenever I wanted a wagon or anything, he'd say, 'Take what you like, Arthur.' If I wanted hay, he'd give it to me. His name was William Arthur Bird and he was a good man.

The bloke that give me all the trouble was only livin' on what he could steal off me. He put a fence right round the lake so he could steal my sheep. Got his son to lift up the bottom fence at the bottom dam and mix my sheep with his. I lost a lot of sheep that way. He used to have meetings at his place, tryin' to be a big shot, sayin' he was the first man with

Corriedale sheep. In the end, he had no Merino at all, only Corriedale...my Corriedale!

When the sheep came back to my land, he summonsed me. I had no earmark on my sheep, only a woolbrand. He put his own earmark on my sheep then accused me of stealin' them. The police came out and saw my Corriedale sheep runnin' back to me.

I went down to Perth and saw a lawyer. When I told him what was going on, he said, 'You let me handle this.' While I was sittin' there, he rang the police.

'What's this I hear about Corunna being accused of stealing sheep?' he said.

I don't know what the policeman said, but my lawyer replied, 'You speak to me like that again, man, and I'll have you in gaol! Any further action on this has to go through me, I'm Corunna's lawyer. We're going to fight you on this!'

After that, they dropped the case against me. They knew they couldn't win. I wasn't stealin' those sheep, they was just comin' home.

No one could ever rightly accuse me of stealin', because everything I got I paid for. I didn't want no one sayin' to me, 'You in debt, we got to sell you up!' You see, they'll get you if they can. They'll follow you to the last ditch, even the government. You got to be a blackfella to know what the pressure is from the government.

Aah, it seems funny, lookin' back now. Mucka was a good place to live in the old days. People were more friendly, they needed each other. The black man was workin' for the farmers, gettin' paid in tea, flour and sugar. Blackfellas cleared the land, put crops in, pulled sandalwood. I remember the lake country used to be full of dingoes, the blackfellas used to track them, hunt them down. Aah yes, no one can say the blackfella didn't do his share of work in Mucka. They helped make it what it is today.

Well, I'd like to finish my story there. That's the important part. I been livin' in Mucka for years now. I got my children all growed up and my farm is comin' along real nice. I still put a crop in and I got my pigs and there's plenty of the wildlife on my place. The wildlife always got a home with me.

I wish I could give advice for the young blackfellas of today, but I can't. Each man has to find his own way.

You see, the trouble is that colonialism isn't over yet. We still have a White Australia policy against the Aborigines. Aah, it's always been the same. They say there's no difference between black and white, we all Australian, that's a lie. I tell you, the black man has nothin', the government's been robbin' him blind for years.

There's so much the whitefellas don't understand. They want us to be assimilated into the white, but we don't want to be. They complain about our land rights, but they don't understand the way we want to live. They say we shouldn't get the land, but the white man's had land rights since this country was invaded, our land rights. Most of the land the Aborigine wants, no white man would touch. The government is like a big dog with a bone with no meat on it. They don't want to live on that land themselves, but they don't want the black man to get it, either. Yet you find somethin' valuable on the land the Aborigine has got and whites are all there with their hands out.

Those Aborigines in the desert, they don't want to live like the white man, owin' this and owin' that. They just want to live their life free, they don't need the white man's law, they got their own. If they want water in the Gibson Desert, they do a rainsong and fill up the places they want. If it's cold, they can bring the warm weather like the wind. They don't need the white man to put them in gaol, they can do their own punishment. They don't have to hunt too hard, the spirits can bring birds to them. Say they want a wild turkey, that turkey will come along, go past them and they can spear it. Kangaroo, too. They don't kill unless they hungry, the white man's the one who kills for sport. Aah, there's so much they don't understand.

Now, if I had been born a white man, my life would have been different. I'd have had an education the proper way. As it is, I got to take my papers to someone who's educated to get me through. Some things aren't understandable to me. Now I got some of my grandchildren educated, they help me.

I'm a great-grandfather now and proud of it. Only thing is, Daisy beats me there, she's got more great-grandchildren than me. I got to catch up with her. I'm proud of my kids, I'm proud of my whole family. Daisy's family and my family, we special, I got healing powers, but Daisy's got them stronger than me. You see, it runs in our family. The spirit is strong in our family. When I die, someone will get my powers. I don't know who. They have to have a good heart, and live a simple life. Otherwise, you're a motor without petrol. Your power comes from above. You can't cure yourself. You got to use that power to help others.

I'm at the end of my story now. To live to ninety, that's an achievement. I haven't really felt the effect of old age, though, of course, the visibility's gone away a bit, but me mind is not so bad. I've had everything a man could want, really. A little bit of sport and a little bit of music. I'm an entertainer. You take me anywhere and I'll join in, could be playing the mouth organ or anything. I'll give it a go. Everybody liked me, that's what beat me, even some of the men I worked for.

Now my life is nearly over, I'm lookin' forward to heaven. I'll have a better time up there. I'll be a little angel, flyin' around, lookin' after stars and planets, doin' the springcleaning. God is the only friend we got. You stick to Him, He's the only one. He's the best mate a man could have. You don't have Him, you don't have no friend at all. You look away from God, you go to ruin. Take the white people in Australia, they brought the religion here with them and the Commandment, Thou Shalt Not Steal, and yet they stole this country. They took it from the innocent. You see, they twisted the religion. That's not the way it's supposed to be.

I look back on my life and think how lucky I am. I'm an old fella now and I got one of my granddaughters lookin' after me. That's something, these days. And I got Daisy's granddaughter writin' my story. It should be someone in the family. It's fittin'.

I got no desires for myself any more. I want to get my land fixed up so my children can get it and I want my story finished. I want everyone to read it. Arthur Corunna's story! I might be famous. You see, it's important, because then maybe they'll understand how hard it's been for the black-fella to live the way he wants. I'm part of history, that's how I look on it.

6

WHERE TO NEXT?

'It's a wonderful story.' Mum had tears in her eyes when she finished reading Arthur's story.

Like me, Mum now felt that at last we had something from the past to hang on to. There was something to be proud of.

However, in an odd way, we also experienced a sense of loss. We were suddenly much more aware of how little we knew about Nan and about the history and experiences of our own family. We were now desperate to learn more, but there appeared to be few obvious leads left.

After much thought, I decided that our best course was to return to Nan and Arthur's birthplace, Corunna Downs.

Paul thought this was a wonderful idea. He loved the North and he also could see no other way forward for us. He hoped we could persuade Nan to go with us.

When I told Mum about the idea, she wasn't very positive. 'You can't go up there. It's a silly idea, you don't know anyone. Nan won't want you to go.'

'Nan doesn't want me to do anything! All my leads have dried up, Mum, that's all there is left, now.'

When I approached Nan about the idea of going up North,

she was disgusted. 'You're like your mother, you like to throw money away. All you'll be lookin' at is dirt. Dirt and scrub.'

I ignored her and said, 'Why don't you come with me? You might meet some of your old mates up there.'

'Haa!' She laughed and shook her head in disbelief, 'I'm too old. Too old to go bush now. You think I got young legs? Look at them!'

'They look all right to me, Nan. They've been holding you up for over seventy years, no reason to think they'll give out on you now. Besides, you'll be in the car most of the time.'

'I don't like cars and I'm too old to go bush. You're chasin' the wind. You go up there and the cyclone'll get you.'

Mum entered the fray. All this time, she'd been quietly observing Nan's reaction. 'Nan's right, Sally,' she said, much to Nan's surprise. 'You shouldn't spend that money just to look at dirt. What will it achieve? There's no one up there we know. What are you going to do, anyway, walk up to strangers in the street and ask them if they knew Daisy or Arthur Corunna?'

'Yep,' I replied. 'I'll take my tape recorder. Who knows what we will find out.'

Mum's face changed from disbelief to laughter in a matter of seconds. 'You're really determined to do this, aren't you?' she said in a rather hoarse voice.

'You know me, Mum.'

'You know,' Mum said wistfully, 'I've always had a hankering to go North.'

'Who said anything about taking you? I mean, all you'd be doing is looking at dirt. You don't want to go two thousand kilometres for that.'

'You're not leaving me here!'

'No, it wouldn't work. You stay here with Nan. I'll go with Paul and the kids.'

'I'm coming and that's that!' she said.

Nan suddenly interrupted. 'You two, you're both nuts! You, Glad, you're like the wind, you blow here and you blow there. You got no mind of your own.'

'Well, Nan, maybe Mum'll chase the cyclones away!'

Over the following weeks, I made arrangements for our trip. We decided to go in the May school holidays. That way the children could come and Paul, who was a teacher, could do most of the driving.

As the weeks passed, Mum became more and more excited. 'Maybe we will learn something,' she said one afternoon as we pored over a map of Western Australia.

'Of course we will, and even if we don't, it's a good holiday.'

'What are you hoping to find at Corunna?'

'Oh, I don't know.' I felt awkward talking about why I wanted to see Corunna, even with Mum. 'I guess I want to see if there are any of the old buildings left. Buildings that might have been there in Nan's day. And I want to look at the land. I want to walk on it. I know that sounds silly, but I want to be there, and imagine what it was like for the people then.'

Mum nodded. There were tears in her eyes. I tended to cover up my feelings with a rather brusque manner, Mum used humour to hide hers. We'd both been very emotional lately.

After a few minutes, Mum said, 'What if they won't let us on the station? We don't know who owns it now. They mightn't like strangers going out there.'

'Well, I'll ring and arrange it before we leave Perth.' I paused. 'It's important to you to see the old place, isn't it, Mum?'

'Yes, very important.'

As the time for us to leave drew near, Nan became more and more outspoken in her opposition. Apart from threatening us with cyclones, flooded rivers and crocodiles, she tried to convince us that while we were away something terrible would happen to her.

'There'll be no one to look after me. It's no use saying the others will check on me, because they won't. Anything could happen to me.'

'Now, Nan, don't be silly,' Mum coaxed. 'You'll have Beryl here.' (Beryl was a friend of Mum's and had looked after Nan before.) 'And Jill and Bill will both be calling in several times during the week. And David and Helen will be able to see you on the weekends. I'm leaving you plenty of money. If you need anything, Beryl will get it up at the shop.'

'You know my heart's not too good, Gladdie, you'll be sorry if you go away and I die.'

'You've been dying ever since I've known you,' Mum said firmly. Nan, sensing that Mum was not going to be moved, shuffled off with her hand over her supposedly weak heart. True to form, she began developing aches and pains the following week, along with other vague symptoms. One morning, she stayed in bed. 'I think this is the beginning of something serious,' she muttered when Mum took her in her breakfast. Poor Mum couldn't help feeling sympathetic, Nan looked so old and, in Mum's mind, really sick.

'I think it's genuine, this time,' she told me despairingly the following evening. 'I think she really has got something wrong with her.'

'You can't make a proper diagnosis without calling the doctor. If she's faking, she'll recover quick smart, and if she's really sick, she should have a doctor look at her.'

'But she always gets so upset when I talk about getting the doctor.'

'Look Mum, how many years has Nan been having these convenient illnesses? Every time you want to go away, she gets sick. Now listen, if she's really sick this time, then of course you can't leave her. But do you want to miss going North just because of a fake illness?'

'Of course I don't. You're right, I've never been firm with her.'

When Mum returned home that night, she told Nan that if she wasn't better in the morning, she was going to call the doctor. Nan was silent.

'I'm very worried about you,' Mum told her. 'You're the only mother I have and I've got to take good care of you. It's no use me going with Sally when you're sick. I'd never forgive myself if something happened to you. If the doctor says it's serious, then I'll stay here and look after you. I just hope they won't put you in hospital, that's all.'

'Are you really going to call the doctor, Glad?' Nan croaked shakily. 'I'm sure I only need rest.'

'You might need medicine, antibiotics or something like that. It's the only way. Now, you snuggle down and I'll bring you in a cup of tea.'

'Don't bother,' Nan pouted. 'I've already had one. I'd be lyin' here thirsty all night if it was up to you.'

'I was only away half an hour — besides, you said you were too weak to get out of bed.'

'I am weak. I had to force myself. Oh, go away and leave me alone, I need my sleep. You always come and bother me when I'm tryin' to sleep.'

Nan's recovery had begun.

Over the next week we organised the last details of our trip. We obtained a video camera to film the trip so that we could show Nan and my brothers and sisters when we returned.

Amber and Blaze were terribly excited. Zeke, their new little brother, was only six weeks old, the only thing that excited him was milk. The children were convinced that going North was as adventurous as exploring deepest, darkest Africa. Nan had convinced them they'd encounter giant snakes and huge crocodiles every step of the way. Blaze had a bit of rope packed in his bag to catch a pet.

For a long time now, I'd been continually reminding Mum that she could take only a minimum of luggage. We were driving up in a small, self-contained camper-van and we needed every inch of space.

The night before we were due to leave, Mum arrived with a station wagon full of gear. Amber and Blaze laughed and laughed when they saw her drive in. Paul failed to see the funny side. He just put his head in his hands, muttered 'I can't believe it ,' and assigned me the task of sorting through it all.

As we hauled everything from the back of her car, I began to make two piles, one necessities, the other luxuries. I tossed the pick, shovel and bucket on the unwanted pile. I was sure Mum would have no luck hunting for gold with that lot. Also on this pile went the shotgun that didn't shoot, two eiderdowns, a sack of potatoes and two suitcases of clothes. Mum had brought an outfit for every occasion imaginable. We realised then that her definition of roughing it was very different to ours. We decided to take the case of apples and the cartons of Instant Mashed Potato, as well as the boxes of dehydrated peas and corn. It seemed a waste not to use them, though we did wonder how on earth we could eat our way through so much.

By late that evening, we'd finished packing.

Five o'clock the following morning, we were on our way.

RETURN TO CORUNNA

By the time we arrived in Port Hedland, we were eager to begin our investigations. We'd been told to look up someone called Jack, as he knew a lot of people in the area and might be able to help us.

As soon as we saw Jack, we liked him. He was an old man and very friendly. I explained who we were and asked if he could tell us anything about the Brockman or Corunna families. We were amazed when he told us that Albert Brockman had been his good friend. They'd worked together for many years.

'Jiggawarra, that was his Aboriginal name, that's what we all called him up here. Now, he had a brother and a sister that were taken away. They never came back. I think the brother was called Arthur.'

'That's right!' I said excitedly, 'and the sister was Daisy — that's my grandmother.'

'Well, I'll be,' he said, with tears in his eyes. 'So you've come back! There's not many come back. I don't think most of them are interested. Fancy, you comin' back after all these years.'

'Are we related to you, then?'

'Well, now, which way do you go by, the blackfella's way or the white man's way?'

'The blackfella's way.'

'Then I'm your grandfather,' he said. 'And your mother would be my nuba*, that means I can marry her.' Mum laughed. We felt excited at discovering even that.

Jack went on to explain that he was, in fact, Nanna's cousin and that his mother's sister had been on Corunna in the very early days and had married one of the people from Corunna.

'I could have been there myself as a young baby,' he added, 'but that's too far back to remember. I was born in 1903 and worked on Corunna from 1924 onwards. Foulkes-Taylor owned it then. They was a real good mob, that Corunna lot, but they slowly started drifting away. They didn't like the boss.'

'What about Lily?' Mum asked, 'did you know her?' Lily was Nan and Arthur's half-sister.

'Oh yes, I knew Lily, she was a good mate of mine. So was her bloke, Big Eadie. He was a Corunna man, too. Aah, we used to have a lot of corroborees in those days. I can't explain to you how it made us feel inside. I loved the singing. Sometimes we'd get a song and it'd last for days. Lily was a good singer, you could hear her voice out high above the others. All those people are gone now. I suppose Arthur and Daisy are dead, too?'

'Arthur is, but my mother is still alive,' replied Mum.

Jack was very moved. 'Why didn't you bring her with you?'

'We tried,' I replied, 'but she reckoned she was too old to come North. Said her legs wouldn't hold her up.'

Jack laughed. 'That's one thing about mulbas**,' he said, 'they can find an excuse for anything! She's one of the last old ones, you know. Gee, I'd like to meet her!'

---

* *nuba*—a person who is in the correct tribal relationship to another person for the purpose of marriage.

** *mulbas* — the Aboriginal people of the Port Hedland/Marble Bar area of Western Australia. (Derived from man or person.)

'Maybe she'll come next time,' I said hopefully. 'Did Lily have any children, Jack?'

'No. She wanted to. She was good with kids. Looked after plenty of kids in her time. She could turn her hand to anything, that woman. How many kids did Daisy have?'

'Only me,' Mum said sadly. 'I'd love to have come from a big family.'

'Ooh, you ask around,' Jack laughed, 'you'll soon have so many relatives you won't know what to do with them. You'd be related to a lot up here.'

'Really?'

'Too right. You might be sorry you come!'

'There was another sister,' I interrupted. 'I think she was full-blood, but died young. Her name was Rosie.'

'That'd be right. A lot of full-bloods died young in those days.'

'I can't believe we've met you,' I sighed. 'All these people have just been names to us. Talking to you makes them real. We didn't think anyone would remember.'

'Aah, mulbas have got long memories. Most around here remember the kids that were taken away. I should have been taken myself, only the policeman gave me a home after my mother died. Then he farmed me out to other people so I was able to stay in the area. I was one of the lucky ones.'

'Did you know a bloke called Maltese Sam?' Mum asked.

'Oh yeah, he's dead now.'

'Could he have been my mother's father?'

'No, no, not him. I couldn't tell you who her father was. Maybe the station-owner. There's plenty of pastoralists got black kids runnin' around.'

I asked Jack if there was anyone else we should talk to.

'You fellas go and see Elsie Brockman, she's your relation, Albert's wife.'

'Are you sure?' Mum asked in astonishment. 'I thought they'd all be dead by now.'

'Oh, Albert's been gone a while, but Elsie's still here. Only be as young as you,' he told Mum. 'Then there's a big mob in Marble Bar you should see, and Tommy Stream in

Nullagine. Any of you fellas speak the language?'

'No,' I replied, 'but Arthur could and Daisy can. They wouldn't teach us.'

'Shame! There's mulbas here know their language and won't speak it. I'm not ashamed of my language. I speak it anywhere, even in front of white people.'

'Do you speak the same language as my mother?' Mum asked.

'I speak four languages. Light and heavy Naml, Balgoo and Nungamarda and Nybali. Your mother's language would be Balgoo, but she would speak Naml, too. All those old ones from Corunna spoke both. Those two languages are very similar.'

Mum and I exchanged glances. We were going to tackle Nan about that when we got home.

'You sure your granny never came back?'

'Not that we know of. Why?'

'Well, I recall meeting a Daisy in '23. I was workin' between Hillside and Corunna at the time. Never seen her before. It was like she appeared outa nowhere. Took her from Hillside to stay at Corunna. She had family there she wanted to visit. Half-caste she was, pretty, too. She was pregnant, baby must have been near due.'

'I don't think it'd be her,' I replied.

'Well, I just wondered.'

I was wondering, too. And hadn't Alice Drake-Brockman said something about Daisy going back to see her mother?

It was all too much. Our heads were spinning, we seemed to be inundated with new information. The children were becoming restless, so Paul suggested that we have some lunch and talk over what to do. We said goodbye to Jack. It seemed awful, leaving him so soon. We promised to call back if we had the opportunity.

Over lunch, we talked about Elsie Brockman. Mum and I both felt it was probably a different person. We reasoned that as Uncle Albert had been the oldest, quite a bit older than Nan, it would be unlikely his wife was only in her fifties. That would have made her, at the very least, thirty years younger than Albert. We decided to go to Marble Bar, instead.

Fortunately for us, we arrived in Marble Bar on pension day. This meant that most of the people were around town. A group of old men were sitting patiently under a tall shady tree in the main street, waiting for the mail to arrive. We parked nearby and walked over and introduced ourselves. Jack had told us to ask for Roy.

'I'm Roy,' replied an elderly man with a snow-white beard. 'What do you want?'

I smiled and held out my hand. 'I'm Sally and this is Paul and my mother, Gladys.' We shook hands all round. 'We're trying to trace our relatives,' I explained. 'They came from Corunna, went by the names of Brockman or Corunna. We heard you worked on Corunna.'

'Not me! I worked on Roy Hill and Hillside, but you'd be related to Jiggawarra, wouldn't you? I worked with him on Hillside, he built the homestead there. A good carpenter. A good man.'

Another older man interrupted. 'Who are these people?' he obviously asked in his own language.

'Brockman people,' Roy replied.

The other smiled. 'Your mob's from Corunna. You'd be related to most of the people round here, one way or another.'

'You lookin' for your mob now?' another asked kindly.

'Yes,' I replied. 'My grandmother was taken from here many years ago.'

'That's right. Hundreds of kids gone from here. Most never come back. We think maybe some of them don't want to come home. Some of those light ones, they don't want to own us dark ones.'

'I saw picture about you lot on TV,' chipped in another. 'It was real sad. People like you, wanderin' around, not knowin' where you come from. Light-coloured ones wanderin' around, not knowin' they black underneath. Good on you for comin' back, I wish you the best.'

'Thank you.' I smiled. 'We are like those people on TV.

We're up here trying to sort ourselves out.' Then, turning back to Roy, I said, 'Did you know Lily?'

'What do you want to know for?'

'She's my Aunty,' Mum said proudly.

Roy was taken aback for a minute.

'Go on, Roy, tell them about Lily,' the others teased.

Roy shook his head. 'I'm not sayin' a word about Lily.' The other men chuckled. Lily was now a closed topic of conversation.

'What about Maltese Sam?' I asked.

'Maltese? He's finished with this world now.'

'I was told he was my grandmother's father, you know, the father of Jiggawarra's sister.'

'No, no, that's not right,' Roy said.

'You got that wrong,' others chorused. 'Who told you that?'

'Oh, just someone I know in Perth.'

'How would they know, they not livin' here,' replied another. 'We all knew Maltese, it's not him, be the wrong age.'

'Do any of you know who her father might have been?' I asked quietly.

There was silence while they all thought, then Roy said, 'Well, she was half-caste, wasn't she?'

'Yes.'

'Then it must have been a white man. Could have been the station-owner. Plenty of black kids belong to them.'

Just then, we were interrupted by a lady in her fifties. 'Who are you people?' she asked as she walked up to our group.

'Brockman people,' Roy said crossly. 'We're talkin' here!'

'You Christian people?' she asked Mum.

'Yes.'

'I knew it,' she replied excitedly, 'I knew it in my heart. I was walkin' down the street when I saw you people here and I said to myself, Doris, they Christian people, they your people. Now, what Brockman mob do you come from?'

'My mother is sister to Albert Brockman,' explained Mum.

'Oh, no! I can't believe it. You're my relations. My Aunty married Albert Brockman.'

'She's not still alive, is she?' I asked quickly.

'Yes, she's livin' in Hedland. She was a lot younger than him.'

Mum and I looked at each other. We were stupid. We should have believed what Jack told us.

'Come home and have a cup of tea with me,' urged Doris. 'I'll ring Elsie and tell her about you, she won't believe it!'

We thanked the men for their help and said goodbye.

Doris made us a cup of tea when we got to her place and we encouraged her to talk about the old days. She said she could just remember Annie, Nan's mother. She thought she'd died somewhere in the 1930s at Shaw River.

'All the old people had a little camp out there,' she explained. 'There was nowhere else for them to go. All the old Corunna mob died out there.'

'Did Lily die out there, too?' Mum asked.

'Yes, she did.'

'Roy wouldn't tell us anything about Lily.'

Doris chuckled. 'That's because she was one of his old girlfriends. He doesn't like to talk about them.' We all laughed.

Just then, another lady popped in. She was introduced to us as Aunty Katy. She was Elsie's sister. We all shook hands and began to talk again.

'Lily was very popular around here,' Aunty Katy told us. 'She could do anything. Everyone liked her, even the white people. She never said "no" to work.'

'How did she die?' Mum asked.

'Now, that's a funny thing,' replied Aunty Katy. 'She came back from work one day and was doing something for one of the old people, when she dropped down dead, just like that! It was a big funeral, even some white people came. Poor old darling, we thought so much of her.'

'She married Big Eadie from Corunna Downs, but there were no children,' added Doris.

'You know, if your grandmother is Daisy, then her grandmother must have been Old Fanny,' said Aunty Katy. 'I'm in my seventies somewhere, but I can remember her, just faintly. She was short, with a very round face, and used to wear a large handkerchief on her head with knots tied all the way around.'

I smiled. Mum just sat there. It was all too much.

Just then, the rest of the family arrived. Trixie, Amy and May. We shook hands, then sat around and had a good yarn. In the process, we learnt that Nan's Aboriginal stepfather had been called Old Chinaman and that he had indeed been a tribal elder on Corunna and had maintained this position of power until the day he died. Also, Annie had had a sister called Dodger, who had married, but never had any children. We also learnt that Albert had been a real trickster, even in his old age.

We all laughed and laughed as funny stories about Albert's pranks kept coming, one after the other. By the end of the afternoon, we felt we knew Albert nearly as well as they did.

Just as the sun was setting, Doris said, 'You fellas should go and see Happy Jack. He knew Lily well. She worked for his family. He lives down near Marble Bar pool.'

We were anxious to learn as much as we could, so we took Doris' advice and headed off in search of Happy Jack.

One look at Jack's place and it was obvious that he was a mechanic. His block was strewn with mechanical bits and pieces, as well as half a dozen Landrovers that he was in the process of fixing.

We explained who we were and showed him some old photos Arthur had given us of the early days. At first he didn't seem to take in what we were saying, but when it finally dawned on him who we were, he was very moved.

'I just can't believe it,' he exclaimed, 'after all these years.'

'I know you don't know us, Jack,' I said, 'but it would mean so much to us if you could tell us about Lily. We know very little and we would like to be able to tell Daisy about her when we go home.'

'I'm happy to tell you anything I know,' he said as we

settled ourselves around his kitchen table. 'She was a wonderful woman. She worked for my family for many years. You know, she's only been dead the better part of fifteen years, what a pity she couldn't have met you all.'

'We wish we'd come sooner,' I replied. 'Doris told us so many of the old ones have died in recent years.'

'That's right. And that Corunna mob, there was some very good people amongst that mob. They were all what you'd call strong characters, and that's by anyone's standard, white or black. Now, my family, we started off most of the tin-mining in this area. We would go through and strip the country, and all that old Corunna mob would come behind and yandy* off the leftovers. I think they did well out of it. We were happy for them to have whatever they found, because they were the people tribally belonging to that area. It was like an unwritten agreement between them and us. Now and then, others would try to muscle in, but we wouldn't have any of that, it belonged to that mob only. We'd let them come in and carry on straight behind the bulldozers. It gave them a living. We were very careful about sacred sites and burial grounds, too. The old men knew this. Sometimes, they would walk up to us and say, "One of our people is buried there." So we would bulldoze around it and leave the area intact.

'Now Lilla — that's what a lot of us called her, not Lily, she was a great friend of my mother's. She worked in the house and was a wonderful cook. Later, when I married, she helped look after my kids. She had a fantastic sense of humour. You could have a joke with her and she'd laugh her head off. All the descendants of that mob are interlocked now, they're all related around here, I can't work it out. It's worse than my own family. What's Daisy like, is she fairly short?'

'Yes.'

'Lilla was like that. Though mind you, in her later years, she became a fairly heavy woman, must have been good pasture she was on. She was wonderful to the old people.

* *yandy* — a process of separating a mineral from alluvium by rocking in a shallow dish.

Even though she was old herself, she worked really hard looking after them. We used to call her The Angel. Some of those old ones at Old Shaw camp couldn't move off their mattresses. That didn't worry Lilla, she'd heave them off and heave them back again. If there was trouble, she'd come and see one of our family, because she knew we were on the radio and could get the Flying Doctor in. You see what I mean, she was a beautiful old woman, a very gentle woman, and when she died I felt very sad.'

'Is there anyone else we could talk to who might help us?' I asked after a few minutes' silence. I was amazed at how steady my voice seemed. All I wanted to do was cry.

'Yes,' replied Jack thoughtfully. 'You should go to the Reserve and see Topsy and Old Nancy. Nancy is well into her nineties and Topsy well into her eighties. I think I remember them saying they were on Corunna very early in the piece, they might know your grandmother, and they were great friends of Lilla's. The only thing is, they speak the language. You'd have to get someone to interpret.'

'Thanks very much,' I said. 'You don't know what this means to us.' We all had tears in our eyes then. While Jack had been speaking of Lilla, it was as though we'd all been transported into the past. As though we'd seen her and talked to her. Lily was a real person to us now. Just like Albert.

'Jack,' I said as we left, 'would you mind if I put what you told me in a book?'

'You put in what you like. I'm very proud to have known Lily. I'm extremely proud to have known that woman. The way she conducted herself, the way she looked after her own people, was wonderful. Your family has missed knowing a wonderful woman.'

'Thanks,' I whispered.

We drove back to the caravan park in silence. Even the children were quiet. We unpacked the van and set up our things for tea. I don't think we'd have cared what we ate. We wouldn't have tasted it. Mum and I couldn't help thinking of all the things we'd learnt about our family. Our family was something to feel proud of. It made us feel good inside, and sad. Later that night, Mum and I sat under the stars, talking.

'I wish I'd known them,' Mum sighed.

'Me too.'

'You seem a bit depressed.'

'I am.'

'What about?'

'Dunno.' That wasn't true. I did know, and Mum knew it. It was just that I needed a few minutes to collect my thoughts so I could explain without breaking down. Finally I said, 'It's Lilla. I feel very close to her in spirit. I feel deprived.'

'How do you mean?'

'Deprived of being able to help her. We could have helped her with those old people. I feel all churned up that she did all that on her own. She never had children — we could have been her children. I mean, when you put together what everyone's said, she was obviously working hard all day and then going out to the camp and looking after the old ones, feeding them...' My voice trailed off.

I tossed and turned that night. The feelings I had about Lilla ran very deep, as though someone had scored my soul with a knife. Too deep to cry. Finally, I turned to my old standby. 'Where is she now?' I asked. 'Where are Lilla and Annie and Rosie and Old Fanny? Where are the women in my family, are they all right? I wish I'd been able to help.' Suddenly, it was as if a window in heaven had been opened and I saw a group of Aboriginal women standing together. They were all looking at me. I knew instinctively it was them. Three adults and a child. Why, that's Rosie, I thought. And then the tears came. As I cried, a voice said gently, 'Stop worrying, they're with Me now.' Within minutes, I was asleep.

The following morning, I awoke refreshed and eager to tackle the Reserve. The deep pain inside of me was slowly fading. It would be a long time before it was completely gone. I never told Mum what I'd seen. I couldn't.

I was, therefore, rather surprised when she took me aside and said quietly, 'What happened to you last night?'

'I don't know what you're talking about.'

'Last night, something important happened to you. You were asleep, or at least I thought you were, then suddenly, I saw you standing with a group of Aboriginal women. I think there were three of them and a child. I knew you were trying to tell me something, something important, but I didn't know what.'

'Oh Mum,' I sobbed, 'it was them!' Her face crumpled. She knew who I meant.

'They're all right, Mum, they're happy.' She just kept nodding her head. Then she covered her face with her hands and walked silently away.

By lunch-time, we'd pulled ourselves together sufficiently to be able to tackle the Reserve. We'd asked an Aboriginal woman called Gladys Lee if she would come and interpret for us. Jack had recommended her. She was very happy to do so.

Armed with our old photos, we went from house to house on the Reserve, asking about Lilla. We drew a blank every time. I couldn't understand it.

Finally, we reached the last house. We stepped up onto the small verandah and Gladys showed the photos to two old ladies, then asked about Lilla. No, they didn't know her. Suddenly, I realised that these two ladies were Topsy and Old Nancy. I asked Gladys to show them the photos again.

Topsy took a closer look. Suddenly she smiled, pointed to a figure in the photo and said, 'Topsy Denmark.' Old Nancy took more of an interest then. After a few minutes, she pointed to the middle figure and said, 'Dr Gillespie.'

I pointed to the photo containing Nanna as a young girl and got them to look at it carefully. Suddenly, there was rapid talking in Balgoo. I couldn't understand a word, but I knew there was excitement in the air. Topsy and Nancy were now very anxious about the whole thing.

Finally, Gladys turned to me with tears in her eyes and said, 'If I had known Daisy's sister was Wonguynon, there would have been no problem.'

'Who's Wonguynon?' I asked.

'That's Lilla's Aboriginal name. We only know her by Wonguynon. I loved her, she looked after me when I was very small. She was related to my father. I am your relation, too.'

Topsy and Nancy began to cry. Soon, we were all hugging one another. Gladys and I had tears in our eyes, but we managed not to break down. Topsy and Nancy pored over all the photos I had, chuckling and laughing and shaking their heads. They explained, through Gladys, that they had been on Corunna when Nan had been taken. They'd all cried then, because they were very close.

'They lived as one family unit in those days,' Gladys explained. 'They lived as a family group with Daisy and Lily and Annie. This makes them very close to you. They are your family. Daisy was sister to them. They call her sister, they love her as a sister.'

By this time, we were all just managing to hold ourselves together. I tried not to look at Gladys as she explained things, because I was keeping a tight lid on my emotions. It wasn't that I would have minded crying, it was just that I knew if I began, I wouldn't be able to stop.

Later, we retraced our steps back down through the Reserve, stopping at each house in turn and asking about Wonguynon. It was totally different, now: open arms, and open hearts. By the time we reached the other end of the Reserve, we'd been hugged and patted and cried over, and told not to forget and to come back.

An old full-blood lady whispered to me, 'You don't know what it means, no one comes back. You don't know what it means that you, with light skin, want to own us.'

We had lumps in our throats the size of tomatoes, then. I wanted desperately to tell her how much it meant to us that they would own us. My mouth wouldn't open. I just hugged her and tried not to sob.

We were all so grateful to Gladys for the kind way she helped us through. Without her, we wouldn't have been able to understand a word. Our lives had been so enriched in the past few days. We wondered if we could contain any more.

The following day, we decided to go to Corunna Downs Station. Doris offered to come with us, as she knew the manager. Also, she was worried we might take the wrong track and get lost.

The track to Corunna was very rough. Apparently, it was the worst it had been for years. After an hour of violently jerking up and down, we rounded a bend and Doris said quickly, 'There's the homestead.'

When we reached the main house, Trevor, the manager, welcomed us. We explained why we were there and he showed us over the house. To our surprise and delight, it was the same one Nan and Arthur had known in their day. We saw where the old kitchen had been, the date palm Nan had talked about, and, farther over in one of the back sheds, the tank machine in which Albert had lost his fingers. I suppose these would be items of no interest to most people, but to us they were terribly important. It was concrete evidence that what Arthur had told us and what Nan had mentioned were all true.

There were no Aboriginal people on Corunna now. It seemed sad, somehow. Mum and I sat down on part of the old fence and looked across to the distant horizon. We were both trying to imagine what it would have been like for the people in the old days. Soft blue hills completely surrounded the station. They seemed to us mystical and magical. We easily imagined Nan, Arthur, Rosie, Lily and Albert, sitting exactly as we were now, looking off into the horizon at the end of the day. Dreaming, thinking.

'This is a beautiful place,' Mum sighed.

I nodded in agreement. 'Why did Nan tell me it was an ugly place? She didn't want me to come. She just doesn't want to be Aboriginal.' We both sat in silence.

We stayed on Corunna until late afternoon, then reluctantly drove back to Marble Bar. We wanted to stay longer, but our time was so limited and we now had many other leads to follow.

We all felt very emotional when we left from Doris' house. She looked sad. She'd rung Aunty Elsie and told her we were coming to see her before we returned to Perth. Doris had also suggested that we see Tommy Stream in Nullagine and Dolly and Billy in Yandeearra.

Just as we were leaving, Doris said, 'You know, I've got a stone from the old days. It's hollow in the middle, they used it for grinding seeds out in the bush. You think Daisy might like that? She'd know what it was. It might mean something to her.'

'I'd love it myself,' replied Mum.

'Me too,' I chipped in.

Doris laughed. 'Take it, then. It's from a time we don't see around here any more. You show it to Daisy, it's fitting she should have it.'

With a mighty heave, Paul picked it up and deposited it in the back of the van.

'Are you sure it'll be all right there, Paul?' Mum asked anxiously.

'It's a rock, Mum.' Paul grinned. 'There's not much you can do to damage a rock.'

Just to be sure, Mum wrapped an old kitchen towel around it to cushion it from any bumps in the road. She wanted to preserve it just the way it was. It was a precious thing.

We kissed everyone goodbye and headed off towards Nullagine. Mum and I were both a bit teary. Nothing was said, but I knew she felt as I did. As if we'd suddenly come home. And now we were leaving again. But we had a sense of place, now.

Tommy Stream was a lovely old man. We explained who we were and why we had come. He told us that he was Nanna's cousin and had been on Corunna Downs when she was taken away.

'I remember,' he said softly, 'I was younger than her, so when she left, I was only a little fella, but all the people cried when she went. They knew she wasn't coming back. My kids would be related to you,' he told Mum. 'They'd be like your cousins.'

Mum asked again about Maltese Sam. It was a ghost from the past she wanted very definitely settled.

'That's not right,' replied Tommy after she suggested he might be Nan's father. 'I knew Maltese, he wasn't her father. I don't know who her father was, but it wasn't him.'

We talked a little more about the old days, and when it began to grow dark, we decided to head back to the Nullagine caravan park. The children were tired and hungry. We thanked Tommy for talking to us. Like Doris, he suggested that we visit Billy and Dolly Swan at Yandeearra, and we decided we would head that way the following morning.

Yandeearra was a long drive, so we set out as early as we could. We telephoned ahead to let the people know we were coming and also to ask permission. We didn't want to intrude. Peter Coppin, the manager, was pleased for us to visit and welcomed us all on our arrival.

Before we met anyone else, an older lady came striding towards us. 'Who are you people?' she asked.

Mum explained who we were. The older lady suddenly broke into a big smile and hugged Mum.

'You're my relations,' she cried. 'Lily was my Aunty, dear old thing. I knew you were my people. When I saw your car, I just knew. Something told me I was going to see some of my old people today. No one said anything to me, I just knew in my heart.' We were amazed. Dolly then pointed to Amber and Blaze and said, 'You see those kids, they got the Corunna stamp on them. Even if you hadn't told me, I could tell just by looking at those kids that you lot belong to that old mob on Corunna.'

Dolly introduced us to Billy and we sat and talked about the early days and who was related to who. He was very pleased that we'd been to see Tommy Stream as well as the Marble Bar people. He explained that others had come through, trying to find out who they belonged to.

'We try to work it out,' he told us kindly, 'we tell them best we can, but some of them we just can't place. And that makes us feel bad, because we think they could belong to us, but we don't know how. Now, I know exactly who you fellas are, I can tell you straight. You belong to a lot of the people here. My children would be your relations. Tommy, he's close, and others, too, then there's some that you're related to but not so close. You still related to them, though.'

We stayed the night at Yandeearra. The following morning, Billy and Dolly said, 'We couldn't sleep. We tossed and turned all night, trying to work out which group you belong to. Tell us about where you from again.'

We went through all that we knew again, very slowly. Then Peter Coppin came over and joined in the discussion. They worked out that Dolly was Aunty to Mum, so the groups could be worked out from there.

'There are four groups,' explained Peter. 'Panaka, Burungu, Carriema and Malinga. These groups extend right through. I can go down as far as Wiluna and know who I'm related to just by saying what group I'm from. Farther up north, they got eight groups. We don't know how they work it out, four is bad enough.' We all laughed.

Then Billy said, 'I think we got it now. You,' he said as he pointed to me, 'must be Burungu, your mother is Panaka, and Paul, we would make him Malinga. Now, this is very important, you don't want to go forgetting this, because we've been trying to work it out ever since you arrived.'

Dolly and Peter agreed that those groups were the ones we belonged to.

'You got it straight?' Billy asked.

'I think so.' I repeated the names.

'Good!' he said, 'because some of the ones that come up here get it all muddled up. We want you to have it straight. It's very important.'

'Now you can come here whenever you like,' Peter said. 'We know who you belong to now. If you ever come and I'm not here and they tell you to go away, you hold your ground. You just tell them your group and who you're related to. You got a right to be here same as the others.'

'That's right,' agreed Billy. 'You got your place now.

We've worked it out. You come as often as you please. There's always a spot here for you all.'

We all felt very moved and honoured that we'd been given our groups. There was no worry about us forgetting, we kept repeating them over and over. It was one more precious thing that added to our sense of belonging.

We were all sad when we left the following day. We'd been very impressed with Yandeearra and the way Peter managed the community. It was a lovely place.

Our next stop was Aunty Elsie's place in Hedland. She had a lovely home overlooking the ocean.

I don't think she could take in who we were at first. She'd had little contact with Arthur and Nan, though Albert had talked about them a lot, she told us. As we talked, things began to fall into place. We were surprised at the likeness of some of Aunty Elsie's grandchildren to our own family. We explained how we thought everyone we were related to must be dead and how we couldn't believe she was really Uncle Albert's wife. Aunty told us that she'd been many years younger than Albert when they'd married. There were four children: Brian, William, Claude and Margaret. Aunty was, in fact, roughly the same age as Mum, so they had a lot in common. We showed her photos of the family and laughed once again about all the tricks Uncle Albert played on everyone. Aunty also told us how Uncle Albert had owned his own truck and what a hard worker he'd been. It was a trait that seemed to run in the family.

By the time we finally left, we'd got to know her really well. Aunty gave us a big fish for our tea. We promised we would come to Hedland again and asked her to visit Perth so she could meet the rest of the family. We felt very full inside when we left. It was like all the little pieces of a huge jigsaw finally fitting together.

The following day, it was time to head back to Perth, but there was one last stop to make. Billy and Dolly had told us to visit Billy Moses at Twelve-mile, just out of Hedland. We were all exhausted by this stage, but we didn't want to miss out on anything, so we gathered together the last remnants of our energy and drove out to Twelve-mile.

When we arrived, we were told that Billy and Alma had gone shopping. Only five minutes had passed when a taxi pulled in, bearing Billy and Alma.

They eyed us curiously, obviously wondering who we were and why we were waiting near their house. I felt embarrassed. What if Billy didn't know us after all? I walked forward and held out my hand. I explained slowly who we were and why we had come. He listened seriously, trying to take in everything I said. Suddenly, his face lit up with a heart-warming smile and he said, 'You my relations! Yes, you've come to the right place. You my people. I am your Nanna's cousin.' There were tears in his eyes. I held his hand warmly. Alma smiled.

We walked back to his house and sat down for a chat. Billy said, 'I can't believe it. Some of my people coming all the way from Perth to visit me. You always come here. You can come and live here, I'm the boss. This is your place, too, remember that.' We began to talk about the old times and Billy explained how he, too, was taken away at a young age.

'I was lucky,' he told us, 'I came back. I made it my business to come back and find out who I belonged to. It was funny, you know, when I first came back, no one round here would talk to me. You see, they weren't sure who I was. They were trying to work it out. I'd walk down the street and they'd just stare at me. Then one day, an old fella came into town, he saw me and recognised me. He spoke up for me and said, that fella belong to us, I know who he is. I know his mother. After that, I never had any trouble. They all talk to me, now. I belong here. It's good to be with my people. I'm glad you've come back.'

We were glad, too. And overwhelmed at the thought that we nearly hadn't come. How deprived we would have been if we had been willing to let things stay as they were. We would have survived, but not as whole people. We would never have known our place.

That afternoon, we reluctantly left for Perth. None of us wanted to go, Paul included. He'd been raised in the North and loved it. We were reluctant to return and pick up the threads of our old lives. We were different people, now. What had begun as a tentative search for knowledge had grown into a spiritual and emotional pilgrimage. We had an Aboriginal consciousness now, and were proud of it.

Mum, in particular, had been very deeply affected by the whole trip. 'To think I nearly missed all this. All my life, I've only been half a person. I don't think I realised how much of me was missing until I came North. Thank God you're stubborn, Sally.'